Fed by the Lord

Fed by the Lord

At-Home Scriptural Formation to Prepare Children for First Communion

Leonard J. DeLorenzo

LITURGICAL PRESS
Collegeville, Minnesota

www.litpress.org

Cover design and mosaic by John Vineyard.

Scripture quotations are from Revised Standard Version Bible, Catholic Edition, copyright © 1965, 1966, Division of Christian Education of the National Council of the Churches of Christ in the United States of America. Used by permission. All rights reserved worldwide.

Scripture quotations are from Jewish Publication Society TANAKH translation, copyright © 1985, 1999 by the Jewish Publication Society. Used by permission. All rights reserved.

Scripture quotation is from the *New American Bible, revised edition* © 2010, 1991, 1986, 1970 Confraternity of Christian Doctrine, Washington, DC and is used by permission of the copyright owner. All Rights Reserved. No part of the New American Bible may be reproduced in any form without permission in writing from the copyright owner.

© 2023 by Leonard J. DeLorenzo
Published by Liturgical Press, Collegeville, Minnesota. All rights reserved. No part of this book may be used or reproduced in any manner whatsoever, except brief quotations in reviews, without written permission of Liturgical Press, Saint John's Abbey, PO Box 7500, Collegeville, MN 56321-7500. Printed in the United States of America.

Library of Congress Cataloging-in-Publication Data

Names: DeLorenzo, Leonard J., author.
Title: Fed by the Lord : at-home scriptural formation to prepare children for first communion / Leonard J. DeLorenzo.
Description: Collegeville, Minnesota : Liturgical Press, [2023] | Summary: "Fed by the Lord provides at-home scriptural formation for children preparing for First Communion. Written for the adults who guide them, this resource focuses on nourishing relationships between children and parents as well as the Lord who feeds them through twelve stories of God feeding his people"—Provided by publisher.
Identifiers: LCCN 2022046793 (print) | LCCN 2022046794 (ebook) | ISBN 9780814668627 (trade paperback) | ISBN 9780814668634 (epub) | ISBN 9780814668634 (pdf)
Subjects: LCSH: First communion—Catholic Church—Study and teaching.
Classification: LCC BX2237 .D45 2023 (print) | LCC BX2237 (ebook) | DDC 264/.02036—dc23/eng/20230109
LC record available at https://lccn.loc.gov/2022046793
LC ebook record available at https://lccn.loc.gov/2022046794

To Tim O'Malley,
who teaches and lives by eucharistic charity

"The eyes of all look hopefully to you;
you give them their food in due season.
You open wide your hand
and satisfy the desire of every living thing."

(Ps 145:15-16, New American Bible, Revised Edition)

Contents

Introduction   1

1. The Human Being and the Garden
   (Gen 2:4-9, 15-17)   9
2. The Forbidden Fruit
   (Gen 3:1-10)   23
3. The Passover
   (Exod 12:1-20)   35
4. The Manna
   (Exod 16:1-35)   44
5. The Prophet's Strength
   (1 Kgs 19:1-21)   52
6. The Abundant Bread
   (2 Kgs 4:42-44)   61
7. Jesus Feeds the Five Thousand
   (Mark 6:30-44)   69
8. Jesus Turns Water to Wine at Cana
   (John 2:1-11)   79
9. Jesus Is the Bread of Life
   (John 6:25-38, 41-42, 48-58)   87
10. Jesus Institutes the Eucharist at the Last Supper
    (Luke 22:1-2, 14-20)   100
11. Jesus Redeems the Two Bound for Emmaus
    (Luke 24:13-37)   110
12. Jesus Renews His Disciples on the Seashore
    (John 21:1-14)   120

Epilogue   127

Introduction

My son Josiah wrote this book with me. On Sunday afternoons for several months during his year of preparation to receive First Communion, we sat at a table in our home and read Scripture together. We started in the Old Testament, selecting six episodes where the Lord feeds his people. We then moved to the gospels, with six more episodes where Jesus brings this divine giving to its completion with the gift of his Body and Blood for his disciples.

With each episode, Josiah and I started in prayer, then we read the passage together. We went back over it so I could ask him questions and he could ask me questions. We would point out the important or surprising things in each episode, and by the later episodes we were making connections to the ones that came before. After our reading and conversation, Josiah would illustrate the episode, then tell me about what he drew and why.

As father and son, we prayed together, studied together, wondered and laughed together. He learned from me a lot that he did not know about how God has acted throughout salvation history, and I learned from him how to stumble over the Word of God with child-like curiosity.

After twelve Sundays focusing on these twelve episodes, with twelve prayerful and fun conversations together, and with twelve of his own drawings giving shape and color to these biblical scenes, we had created the basis of this book. Of course, much more than a book was being created during this time. Most of all, paying attention to these particular actions throughout Scripture created one firm, clear, and beautiful memory for Josiah: the Lord feeds his people. Even more, when Josiah stepped forward to receive his First Communion on

May 16, 2020, he rejoiced at the wonder that now he himself was being fed by the Lord.

Investing in You, Who Invest in Your Child

This book comes from the desire to equip and empower parents and mentors to provide their children with a biblically rich preparation for First Communion. Young people do not need more programs; what they need is more meaningful connections. This simple but substantive approach fosters two crucial connections for young people:

- First, they connect with their parents or other mentors who spend time with them in a focused way to read and learn, pray and talk.
- Second, young people connect with the Word of God—Jesus Christ—who reveals himself to us in Scripture and comes to us personally in the Eucharist.

With these connections in mind, my goal is to help nourish and support you, the adult reader of this book. I want to nourish you by giving you the opportunity to further develop your own biblical imagination, and I want to support you as you guide your child or student toward an intimate encounter with the Lord. Everything presented here is meant to foster relationship: between you and the Lord, you and your child, your child and the Lord who feeds us.

This formation allows young people preparing for First Communion to recognize and wonder at how God feeds his people. When we receive the Body and Blood of Christ, God is feeding us in the most personal and intimate way. It is important that young people know that. It is even more important that they trust in this most wondrous gift. We must help every young person who receives the Eucharist to believe in their mind but especially in their heart that *this is God, feeding me*.[1]

---

[1] According to one recent study, the majority of Catholics do not believe the Eucharist is the Body and Blood of Christ. Renewed belief in the Lord's presence can begin from the direct and personal trust that when you receive the Eucharist, the Lord is feeding you. See Gregory A. Smith, "Just One-Third of U.S. Catholics Agree with Their Church That Eucharist Is Body, Blood of Christ," *Pew Research Center*, August 5, 2019, https://www.pewresearch.org/2019/08/05/transubstantiation-eucharist-u-s-catholics/.

By spending time with the twelve episodes of this biblical journey, we see that it is characteristic of God to feed his people. In other words, this is just what God does: God feeds. This is no distant or remote god; rather, this is the God who draws near and cares for us. He gives us what we need. Since what we need above all is him, he gives us himself as our daily bread. To know God is to know him as the one who gives life, who nourishes us, who cares for us. This is who God is. By studying together the actions of God in Scripture, we prepare our children to make a remarkable act of faith: to believe that *when I receive the Eucharist, I am being fed by God.* That one, simple belief opens them to being changed, just as it should open us to being changed over and over again.

One of the surest ways to incite wonder and love for the Lord in our children is for us to rekindle wonder and love for the Lord in ourselves. We have a responsibility to instruct our children—to model and share our faith with them. For many of us, this begins as a daunting and uncertain task: we might question our own faith, or feel awkward in our wording or mannerisms in sharing faith, or recognize our own lack of knowledge when it comes to Scripture or the particularities of Catholic doctrine. I had all this in mind as I prepared this book for you, especially because I felt all those things myself when it was time for me to begin forming my children to reverence our eucharistic Lord and welcome him in the Blessed Sacrament. That is why this book is first of all an investment in you, to nourish and guide you, so that you may nourish and guide your children with greater confidence and joy.

Growing Accustomed to the Ways of God

St. Jerome, who translated the Bible into Latin in the fourth century, famously wrote that "Ignorance of Scripture is ignorance of Christ." Why is that? Because Christ is the one through whom, with whom, and in whom all things are created. He is God's saving action. He is the fulfillment of the Law and the Prophets. He is God-with-us. To know him for who he is, as he is, means growing in knowledge of how God creates, how God speaks and acts, and how God reveals himself through history and especially to the people of Israel. To know him who fulfills the Law, we need to learn about the Law; to know him who completes prophecy, we must study what is prophesied. Without becoming more and more immersed in Scripture throughout our lives, who Jesus really is may become fuzzy and vague, even to the point that we create the Lord in our own image of what we *think* God is or should be, rather than letting God be God and allowing our hearts and minds to be transformed by him. If ignorance of Scripture is ignorance of Christ, then familiarity with Scripture forms us for intimacy with Christ as he is.

The twelve biblical episodes in this approach to sacramental preparation guide us—and then the children we form—to become more familiar with God's actions and thus with God's "character," if you will. We will ponder even those episodes that are familiar to us with fresh eyes, noticing details that might have eluded us previously, slowly allowing connections to emerge, and moving beyond first impressions. Six of these episodes come from the Old Testament, where Jesus Christ is not named explicitly:

- The Human Being and the Garden (Gen 2:4-9, 15-17)
- The Forbidden Fruit (Gen 3:1-10)
- The Passover (Exod 12:1-20)
- The Manna (Exod 16:1-35)
- The Prophet's Strength (1 Kgs 19:1-21)
- The Abundant Bread (2 Kgs 4:42-44)

These Old Testament episodes ultimately reveal ways in which Christ is anticipated and prefigured, though we will not fully see that until we turn our attention to the six gospel episodes that come later. In these gospel episodes, Jesus Christ is front and center:

- Jesus Feeds the Five Thousand (Mark 6:30-44)
- Jesus Turns Water to Wine at Cana (John 2:1-11)
- Jesus is the Bread of Life (John 6:25-38, 41-42, 48-58)
- Jesus Institutes the Eucharist at the Last Supper (Luke 22:1-2, 14-20)
- Jesus Redeems the Two Bound for Emmaus (Luke 24:13-37)
- Jesus Renews his Disciples on the Seashore (John 21:1-14)

What is happening as we and our children pay attention to each of these episodes is certainly that we are learning *what* the Bible says. Beyond this, though, we are also learning *how* to read the Bible. When you develop a really close relationship with a friend over a long period of time, you end up paying attention to a lot of the things this person says and does—you learn about them through their words and actions. But your knowledge of them—your relationship with them—is not just about the accumulation of all these experiences and memories of what they say and do; even more, you become formed to *how* this person thinks, judges, values, and operates. You just "get each other." That is an analogy for the relationship and distinction between learning *what* the Bible says and *how* to read the Bible. Over time and with devoted attention, we slowly move from learning about these different events of God to "getting" who our God is. We just "get him" like he "gets us." Knowledge becomes understanding, and understanding opens us further to love.

How This Works

In a previous book titled *Turn to the Lord: Forming Disciples for Lifelong Conversion* (Liturgical Press, 2021), I presented a new approach to forming people for the completion of Christian initiation, principally through preparation for the sacrament of confirmation. That approach was designed for groups from parishes or schools, under the direction of parents and other mentors. The approach I am presenting in this book is similar to that other approach in that both depend on scriptural immersion, the development of meaningful relationships, and the integration of what we learn with how we live. What is different in the First Communion version is that this is more of a one-on-one approach, whereas the previous approach for confirmation is intended for and necessitates groups. Together, though, these two approaches aim at more holistic, substantive, enjoyable, and lasting forms of sacramental preparation, with each suited to the specific needs and capacities of those being formed, whether younger children as here, or teenagers, young adults, or even more mature adults in confirmation. What these two approaches also share in common is that both call for and depend on the investment of parents, mentors, and other more mature disciples to be the primary guides and educators.

In each of the chapters that follow, you will find two parts. The first part will be me writing directly to you, bringing us through the specific biblical episodes. This is for your own enrichment and nourishment. The Dominicans, as the Order of Preachers, have a saying about their religious charism: each of them is like "one beggar telling another beggar where they have found bread." We can think of the first part of each chapter in similar terms: I'm the first beggar who has found great sustenance in each of these biblical episodes, thanks in no small part to what others have shown me in their own teaching and writing. You are the best resource and most persuasive mentor for the child you will be teaching and forming. The first part of each chapter is an investment in you.

The second part of each chapter, then, is a guide for how you might lead a session with your child. In my experience, each session takes from forty-five to sixty minutes. That includes time to pray together, slowly read the passage together, and talk and ask questions about the passage. It also includes time for your child to draw and color the scene on their own, or to engage in some other kind of creative or reflective activity. I will point out some alternative possibilities to drawing and coloring at the end of the first session, though I consider the drawing-and-coloring activity to be the best. One of the distinctive and beautiful benefits I have found in having my children draw the scenes that we study together is that later in the year we would go back to earlier scenes and my child would describe his or her drawing to me. In doing so, they would recall the biblical episodes in quite considerable detail. As necessary, I could then ask questions about the drawing with specific main points about the biblical scene in mind, and because my children were looking at something they created, they had a better chance of not only remembering but also being able to tell me about that point in their own words.

When I have followed this approach with my own children (I am now doing it for the third time), we would study one of these scenes (i.e., one "session") each weekend. For us, this never came out to twelve straight weekends of this kind of formation. More typically, we would have three or four weekends in a row, then a weekend or two of something else, then back for a few more consecutive weekends. At the end of these twelve sessions, we also took at least one additional weekend to look at everything together (my kids' drawings are amazingly helpful for this), which inevitably leads us even more to learn about and marvel at how the Lord feeds us.

On the weekends when we were not engaging in this particular form of preparation, we took on other intentional practices to prepare for First Communion. This is very fitting since this "fed-by-the-Lord" formation is meant to be a main piece of a young person's preparation for receiving the sacrament, but not the exclusive means of formation. This formation should be accompanied by instruction and immersion in prayer, time spent in Eucharistic Adoration, preparation for First Reconciliation, and potentially some retreat experience with a parish community. I worked with my parish director of religious education when developing this approach, and in our case this served in place of my children attending the traditional religious education classes at our parish; however, this way of formation may very well be a supplement to the formation and education that occurs in parish- or school-based faith formation curricula. Whether or not children are enrolled in a group or class for First Communion preparation, the distinctiveness of this approach is precisely in the guidance and empowerment afforded to parents to directly engage with their children in religious formation. This type of investment in the formation of our young people should be one of the foundational and totally common parts of religious education and sacramental preparation: an investment in a relational approach to biblical catechesis.

As you prepare to immerse yourself in these wondrous mysteries of God's care for us, I hope and pray that what I offer in the pages to follow will nourish your mind and fill your heart. To the extent that something like that happens, it will not be I who is nourishing and filling you, but indeed our Lord, the Incarnate Word, who is giving himself to you and preparing you to receive him ever more generously and gratefully. As parents and teachers, catechists and mentors, we hope for nothing less for our own children as we are called to take up our irreplaceable responsibility in passing on a living faith to them. At the end of all our hopes and labors, all our successes and even our failures, we are ultimately called to let our children walk on their own to the altar where the Lord of all comes to meet them, personally. We will have done well if, when they open their mouths to receive the Eucharist, they are ready to believe that right then and there, they themselves are being fed by the Lord.

chapter one

The Human Being and the Garden

(Gen 2:4-9, 15-17)

What takes place in the Garden of Eden is a children's story. It is simple and direct, earthy and homey, familiar and personal. This is the kind of story that adults might read to children but not one that adults read seriously for themselves. To many adults, this story seems childish.

C. S. Lewis was the author of one of the greatest works of children's literature of the twentieth century, The Chronicles of Narnia. He wrote the first chronicle for his goddaughter, who was then a child. He knew that by the time it was published, his goddaughter would think herself too old for a children's story. In a letter to her, he said that someday she would be old enough to read this story again.[1] He meant that once adults reach a certain level of maturity, they might allow themselves to enjoy again things that they would have enjoyed as children but thereafter considered beneath them.

That is a strange cycle, if you think about it. It is as if there is a stage of immaturity in adulthood when we consider ourselves too smart, too sophisticated, too grownup to take seriously things that seemed suited to us as children. Of course, there are things you do as a child

---

[1] C. S. Lewis, *The Lion, the Witch and the Wardrobe*, The Chronicles of Narnia (New York: HarperCollins, 2001), 110.

that you should *not* do as an adult—especially in your later years—like trying to run up a slide at full speed. That ceases to be fun when it's the fast-track to dislocated knees.

But aren't the best children's stories the ones that come back to us with remarkable relevance after we've passed through the immaturities of our nascent adulthood? *The Giving Tree* delights, haunts, and soothes the seasoned parent reading it to her youngest child. *The Velveteen Rabbit* is like something remembered from ages past while also being something strangely new at the same time. The same could be said of *The Lion, the Witch and the Wardrobe*, or any of Lewis's chronicles. As Lewis himself observed: "A children's story which is enjoyed only by children is a bad children's story. . . . No book is really worth reading at the age of ten which is not equally (and often far more) worth reading at the age of fifty—except, of course, books of information."[2]

Is the creation account in Genesis 2 like a book of information? If it were, then it would indeed be the kind of thing that you read as a child until you grasp the basics, then leave behind, only to be of interest again for the sake of reading to a child for their own good, but no longer for your own. If we as adults, however, would be willing to suspend our judgment long enough to at least entertain the possibility that this story might be something equally worth reading at age fifty as at ten, then perhaps we would find two *very* adult questions addressed in the narrative right from the start: "Who am I?" and "Where am I?"

It may just be that this is a children's story that we never outgrow, or rather one that we grow into over and over again.

Who Am I?

The question of who I am reaches far and wide, but it fundamentally begins with the question of *what* I am—me, this human being. Without any beating around the bush (that comes later in Genesis 3:8-10), this account goes straight away to the fundamental claim about what a human being is: "The LORD God formed man from the dust of the

---

[2] C. S. Lewis, *Of Other Worlds: Essays and Stories* (San Diego: Harcourt, 1994), 15, 24.

earth. He blew into his nostrils the breath of life, and man became a living being" (Gen 2:7).[3]

There are three parts to this one verse. First, there is the action of the LORD God to form and shape "man" out of the dust of the earth. Like a potter working with unformed clay, the Creator fashions a body from this earthy stuff. The relationship between the body that is formed and the stuff from which it is formed is in fact expressed in the original Hebrew of this verse, though we do not always capture that connection in English (or other languages in translation). The word "man" is the translation of the Hebrew term *'adam*, which is not yet the proper name "Adam." That term is related to the Hebrew word translated here as "earth," which is *'adamah*. The "man" is the earth creature: the one formed from the earth.[4]

Second, the LORD God breathes his own breath into the creature he has fashioned from the earth. It is difficult if not impossible to imagine a more intimate action than this. The Creator gives what is his own to his creature so that the creature may be filled with what was not his own but becomes his own by this gift. We do well to wonder at how close the LORD God is to his creature here as he breathes into him. The LORD God both holds this creature in his hands as he forms him and touches his creature with his lips as he offers his breath.

Third, the "man"—the one formed from the earth—becomes a living being. Notice that it is not the fashioning of the body that makes him a living being, nor is it the giving of breath that makes him a living being. It is only the *union* of the formed earth stuff and the donated breath that makes *'adam* a living being. This is the third and ultimate action of the Creator: to bring together and join what were otherwise separate. Here we see the union of body and soul as the living human being. The human being is never less than or other than this—to be a human being is to be a living union.

---

[3] All biblical quotations in this chapter come from the Jewish Publication Society (JPS) translation, unless otherwise noted.

[4] In his translation of the verse, Robert Alter seeks to preserve more of the connection present in the Hebrew when rendered into English by describing the "human" as "humus from the soil" in *The Five Books of Moses: A Translation with Commentary* (New York: W. W. Norton, 2004), 21.

As adults more than as children, we forget or we deny—or we *are* denied—what we are. It is tempting to think (or be persuaded that) "I am *not* my body"—this stuff, this baggage, these wounds and limitations and marks and history. It is tempting to think that the "real me" is separate from my body. Alternatively, it is tempting to think (or be persuaded) that what animates me and gives me life is what I choose or make for myself, or what others validate in me, or what passes as favorable in this time or that. Yet here comes this "children's story" to state quite directly and conclusively that I—this human being—am fundamentally and inerasably the living union of body and soul: a body fashioned by the Lord God, a soul given by the Lord God. It would be easier to choose one or the other, to define myself by *just this* or *just that*. But we are challenged to hold both, and to see the gift of that union as true for ourselves and for each other.[5]

Where Am I?

War, violence, hatred, cruelty, greed, malnourishment, drought, floods, famine, wildfires, and deception upon deception upon deception. To look around our world or to see what passes through the news before it is replaced by something else creates the overwhelming impression that *this* world is anything but good. It often feels like we ought to get away from this place, separate ourselves from what happens here, and find security somewhere else, in some other way. On the individual level and the societal level, I suspect we all know that deep, piercing question: "Where am I?"

Once again, the creation account of Genesis 2 does not dally or delay, but gets right to a fundamental claim about what this world of ours really is. Immediately after the verse about the creation of the human being as the union of intentionally formed earth stuff and divine breath, we read this:

---

[5] For a robust and compelling account of how this fundamental claim about the wholeness of the human being as the union of body and soul establishes the basis of a Christian response to more modern "gender paradigms," see, for example, Abigail R. Favale, *The Genesis of Gender: A Christian Theory* (San Francisco: Ignatius, 2022).

> The LORD God planted a garden in Eden, in the east, and placed there the man whom He had formed. And from the ground the LORD God caused to grow every tree that was pleasing to the sight and good for food, with the tree of life in the middle of the garden, and the tree of knowledge of good and bad. (Gen 2:8-9)

The LORD God, who intentionally and intimately creates the human being, places his creature in a garden full of what will nourish and delight him. This is a statement about the world—*our* world—the world which the LORD God creates. We are placed in a world that is made to sustain us and provide us with our basic needs. This account suggests to us that before all the complexities of human life come into play, we are creatures who depend on what is around us, available to us, and given to us for our daily existence. *This* world that the LORD God creates and in which he has placed us was, from the very beginning, such a world.

The scholar Leon Kass, in reflecting on this passage and noticing how the very simplicities of human life are accounted for here, sees how this second creation account speaks personally to each of us who begin our lives in innocence and infancy:

> Whatever else human beings are or become, they are, always and at bottom, *also* beings with an uncomplicated, innocent attachment to their own survival and ease, beings who experience and feel, immediately and without reflection, the goodness of their own aliveness. . . . From the point of view of simple necessity—for food and drink—the world is a rather generous place; were it not for the depredations of civilized man, it would be so still. For many of our simpler relatives, including primates, it remains in large measure a veritable garden; and it would still be so for us, had we never risen up from animality—or for that matter, from childhood.[6]

This is not a political statement. It is rather a statement about the goodness of creation, something we hear repeated over and over again—seven times—in the first creation account of Genesis which precedes this one. The world is good; it is created good; it is a good

---

[6] Leon R. Kass, *The Beginning of Wisdom: Reading Genesis* (Chicago: University of Chicago Press, 2006), 60.

place for us. However bad things might get, the world is still good, as God's creation.

Our first experiences of life are experiences of the goodness of the world. We do not bring ourselves into existence but are rather placed in this world, much like the Lord God placed his *'adam* in Eden. We are given sustenance before we even know we need it. We find warmth in the womb before we know cold. Oxygen fills our lungs without gasping for it. As we grow older and become so occupied and preoccupied with all the things we lack or want or need, we tend to forget just how much we are provided for simply by being in this world.

In seeing infants or even contemplating children in the womb now, all of us may recognize or reimagine this remarkable state of existence: we begin life by receiving and, by and large, our first experience of life in this world is of a world that provides for us.[7] When we read the creation account in Genesis 2, Leon Kass says that "we experience the original *'adam* as a grown-up child enjoying the pleasures of a childlike existence."[8] Maybe we are nostalgic for that, even if most of us would not choose to become an infant again. Nevertheless, do we not encounter in this image of the original *'adam* something of what we hope for and cherish in our own children? We want to give them what they need. We guard their innocence even though we know they will change and become more complicated. This biblical account echoes back to us our own longings for our children: that they may have life and nourishment and security and peace.

The Garden of Eden is not primarily about what we have "lost"; it is, rather and more deeply, about what the world fundamentally is, as the Lord God's creation. The garden is a gift and it is filled with gifts. This is the world the Lord God creates *for us*. So that we may live well in the world, the Lord God gives us not only what we need but also instruction in how to live here well:

> The Lord God took the man and placed him in the garden of Eden, to till it and tend it. And the Lord God commanded the man, saying, "Of every tree of the garden you are free to eat; but as for the tree of knowledge of good and bad, you must not eat of it; for as soon as you eat of it, you shall die." (Gen 2:15-17)

---

[7] St. Augustine offers a marvelous reflection on infancy in *The Confessions*, I.6.7, trans. Maria Boulding (New York: Vintage, 1998), 7.

[8] Kass, *Beginning of Wisdom*, 61.

We ought not jump ahead too quickly because we happen to *know* what happens in the next chapter. Instead, we should pause and pay close attention to this one instruction, this one commandment. Did you notice that it is overwhelmingly positive? *Everything* is given to 'adam to eat, everything but this *one* thing. Yes, indeed, that one thing is where the drama to come unfolds (and we'll get to that), but we might be so consumed with that idea from the start that we miss a really crucial thing: everything is given.

It is also important to recognize that there are two trees in the middle of the garden (see Gen 2:9). When most of us recall this narrative from memory, it is only the tree of the knowledge of good and bad that is in the middle. Isn't that funny? We make the forbidden thing the center of everything. At minimum, though, we should see that the tree of life is the first one mentioned as being in the middle of the garden, where the tree of the knowledge of good and bad also is. An array of other trees surrounds these two trees, giving nourishment and delight to the creature the Lord God has created.

Who Is God?

To look back over just these several verses from Genesis 2, we might discover not only the two very adult questions of "Who am I?" and "Where am I?" but yet another question equally profound and expansive: "Who is God?" Rather than conjure up answers on our own, let us see what we can see in the text itself:

- God is the one who gives water when the land is dry (2:5).
- God is the one who shapes and forms (2:7a).
- God is the one who gives his breath (2:7b).
- God is the one who makes us into living beings (2:7c).
- God is the one who creates a world that supports our needs (2:8-9).
- God is the one who tells us how we are to live, for our own good (2:16-17).

When, as Christians, we pray in the Lord's prayer that "Our Father . . . give us this day our daily bread," we pray that the Lord will do for us today what the Lord has done for us from the beginning of our lives: care for us, provide for us, feed us. This "children's story" is about all the most important things: who we are, where we are, and who God is. To forget any one of those things is to get life all wrong. Getting life right often requires us to return to the basics, becoming children again.

Guiding Your Child to Engage "The Human Being and the Garden"

Overview

A Look from Above
For each session, I will use this "look from above" to give us a sense of perspective and context within the whole. I will often mention connections to the sessions that immediately preceded the present one, or, especially when we get to the gospel episodes, to sessions that came quite a bit earlier in our journey. With this being the first session, there are not yet other sessions to connect to, though what we explore together here relates to every other session that comes after. This is part of the approach of this formation: we are learning to see each of these episodes of the biblical narrative as a whole, bringing to light God's continuous action of care for us. In what follows, I am offering a basic and repeatable pattern for sharing time with your child, being immersed together in this narrative of being fed by the Lord. You may of course find that variations on this pattern work best for you and your child, so please feel free to adapt and adjust as necessary. This particular episode will later connect to Jesus preparing breakfast for his disciples on the seashore (chapter 12).

A Closer Look
The "closer look" is an occasion for introducing this particular session more specifically. In addition to focusing on the particular biblical episode in this session, we also want to set the foundation for the routine we will follow in all of the sessions of this formation. This is all new to your child, so getting comfortable with this basic routine will help them in the weeks and months to come to engage what we are doing more naturally. The content for this particular session comes from the second creation account (Gen 2) where we want to pay attention to three things: (1) how the Lord God creates human beings and what human beings are; (2) what the garden is like and connect that to the world the Lord God creates for us; (3) how we would receive what the Lord God gives to us, rather than taking something—for example, what it looks like to *receive* rather than *take*.

18 *Fed by the Lord*

1ˢᵗ Movement—Welcoming the Word of God

1. Opening Prayer

   All throughout these sessions together, it is usually best to offer a personal prayer spoken directly to God asking him to open our hearts and minds, helping us to see how he feeds us. The more personal this prayer is, the better. In time, it is also good to ask your child to offer a little prayer out loud at the beginning, or you can dedicate a bit of time (even ten seconds) to silence as part of that opening prayer. You may like to conclude this short opening prayer with the Our Father or ask for the intercession of the Blessed Mother with a Hail Mary. The most important thing is to open each session with prayer, asking God for his grace and guidance. This is sacred time spent together in the Lord's presence.

2. Quick Review

   In all of the sessions to come, it will be helpful and important to review one or more of the previous sessions. One of the best ways to do this is to look together at the art that your child created for that session, or, alternatively, go over together the other activity they did in place of the art. Since this is the first session, there is obviously nothing to review from earlier.

2ⁿᵈ Movement—Engaging the Word of God

1. Reading

   Genesis 2:4-9, 15-17.

   Read the passage through slowly. You will likely be the one reading, but maybe your child is capable and willing to read aloud instead. Either way, read the passage out loud together.

   If you are wondering which Bible to use, there are certainly many options. My children and I often used *The Saint John's Bible*, which is beautifully illuminated and filled with enriching illustrations.[9] That Bible is available in seven different volumes, making it a bit of an investment. Throughout this book you will see that I tend to use

---

[9] *The Saint John's Bible*, 7 vols. (Collegeville, MN: Liturgical Press, 2005–2012).

the translation of the Jewish Publication Society (JPS) for the Old Testament[10] and the Revised Standard Version (RSV) for the New Testament.[11] That does not mean you have to have two different Bibles; instead, find a Bible that works for you and your child together. You might appreciate having some commentary in the Bible—that is up to you. The only thing I would caution against is using a "children's Bible" that reduces or summarizes the actual biblical text. Not every children's Bible does that, but some do.

2. Questions about the Reading

After you finish reading the passage once, ask your child questions like the ones below. The idea here is that you ask questions and then go back to the passage to try to find answers together. But your child might also have some responses to the questions you ask before returning to the text a second time—that is all well and good. Just be sure to go back to the passage to either confirm or strengthen or correct yourselves together. This is the time for talking about the passage together, because you are both learning about this (even though you are guiding your child). Be curious and encourage them to be curious, too.

- Ask: How does God create us (i.e., human beings)? (See 2:7-8.)
    - Pay attention to how God intentionally forms the body of the human being from the clay of the earth.
    - Pay attention to how God breathes life into the human being.
    - Pay attention to how God creates us as *both* formed body and given breath.
- Ask: What is the garden like where God places this human being? (See 2:8-9.)
    - Notice how in this garden God causes trees to grow that give food.

---

[10] Adele Berlin and Marc Zvi Brettler, eds., and Michael Fishbane, consulting ed., *The Jewish Study Bible* (Oxford: Oxford University Press, 2004).

[11] *The Ignatius Catholic Study Bible: The New Testament* (San Francisco: Ignatius, 2010).

- Notice how there are two trees in the middle of the many, many trees in this garden: one that is the "tree of life" and another that is "the tree of knowledge of good and bad."
- Ask: What does God tell his creature about eating the fruit of the trees? (See 2:15-17.)
  - See that the human being may eat from *every* tree.
  - See that the human being may *not* eat from *one* tree: the tree of knowledge of good and bad.
  - See how everything is given as a gift, except for what comes from this *one* tree.
- Ask: Almost everything in this garden is a gift. What would you do with your hands if you were receiving a gift from someone?
  - Answer: To receive a gift, you open your hands to receive. Your child might even put one hand under the other and open them up. If they don't, you might suggest that. These are like hands that receive the Eucharist: open and waiting.
- Ask: There is one tree that the human being is not supposed to eat from. What would you do with your hands if you were taking something?
  - Answer: To take something, you likely grab or snatch at it. This movement of your hands is very different from that of receiving.
  - Point: The idea here is to contrast hands that receive (think hands that receive the Eucharist) and hands that take (think, maybe, of swiping something quickly from a store shelf, to steal).

3. Points to Emphasize

After you have finished reading and talking about this passage together with the aid of the questions above, be sure to emphasize the points below in the way you think is best. You might find that you and your child already emphasized these points well when you were talking about the passage—that's great. These are like the "takeaways" from this passage:

- God creates us in a very special (or intentional) way: he forms our bodies and gives us his own breath so we can live.
- God creates a world for us to live in that is filled with gifts for us. It is like a garden.
- There are *two* trees in the middle of the garden: the tree of life, and the tree of the knowledge of good and bad. The only tree from which the human being is told not to eat is the tree of the knowledge of good and bad.
- When you receive a gift, you open your hands. When you take something you're not supposed to, you grab with your hands. When we receive the Eucharist we open our hands because we are receiving a gift.

3rd Movement—Reflecting on the Word of God

1. Activity

    Draw the scene. This is the recommended activity for your child, provided they are open to drawing (and coloring). You might help them think about what part of the scene they would like to draw. It is important not to force ideas on them but rather let them see this on their own, in their own imagination, based on what they encountered in Scripture.

    Alternative activities, for this session or the ones to follow (note: I strongly recommend the drawing-and-coloring activity, if possible):

    - Create a journal in which you write a letter to the Lord each week.
    - Create a banner with a key word from the passage, and decorate it.
    - Use molding clay to shape something from the passage.
    - Write a letter to someone else telling them about what you learned.

- Choose three to five important words or short phrases from the passage and combine them on one sheet as "word art"—for example, write them out and decorate them.

2. Discussion

   Ask your child to tell you about the drawing. Ask questions about it. This is a chance for your child to teach you.

3. Closing Prayer

   Close with a prayer of thanksgiving for your time together. If you want to adopt a regular prayer for the end of the sessions, you might consider a prayer to prepare to receive the Eucharist, like this one:

   Dear Jesus.

   We love you.
   Help us to love you more.
   Thank you for speaking to us in Scripture.
   Thank you for feeding us with your Body and Blood.
   Help us to receive you in love.

   Amen.

chapter two

The Forbidden Fruit

(Gen 3:1-10)

Genesis 3 is the story of the Fall, where sin comes into the world. It is someone else's fault. It is the fault of the first man, not me. It is the fault of the woman who first took the fruit, not me. It is the fault of the serpent who tempted them, not me. Maybe it is even the fault of the LORD God who put that tree there in the first place and who must have created that serpent. Whatever this story is about, it is not about me, even if I believe that I suffer the consequences of what happens here.

You know what's really surprising, though? The impulse to defend myself—the "it wasn't me" defense—is also part of the story. The man blames the woman as he tells the LORD God it wasn't him (3:12), and the woman blames the serpent (3:13). Genesis 3 is the story of the Fall, and it is also the story of how we are reluctant or unwilling to see this as being about ourselves.

The setting is still the garden—the same garden the LORD God created, filled with all manner of fruit-bearing trees. The LORD God has now made a companion for his *'adam*, directly and intimately created from the side of the first, undivided "man." The man rejoices over his companion, names her in reference to himself (*'ishshah*: "woman," very much like "wife"), and even renames himself in reference to her (*'ish*: a different word for "man," very much like "husband").

They live together as one in the LORD God's good garden: naked, without shame (see Gen 2:18-25).[1]

It is important to remember how the LORD God told his *'adam* to live in this Edenic world: "Of every tree of the garden you are free to eat; but as for the tree of knowledge of good and bad, you must not eat of it; for as soon as you eat of it, you shall die" (Gen 2:16b-17).[2] Everything is given, only one thing forbidden. The woman is not yet created when the command is given, so the man must hand on this commandment to her (or, you might consider that they are both there in undivided fashion to receive the commandment, and so they must remember this commandment together as one). In any event, life is good.

The Serpent Speaks

Life *was* good, until the serpent enters the scene and speaks. To this point, all the speech has either been from the LORD God, or from the *'adam* who names the animals and later rejoices at the creation of his companion. When the serpent speaks, he asks a question:

> "Did God really say: You shall not eat of any tree of the garden?" (Gen 3:1)

Things just changed. All we have to do to recognize the change is pause for a moment and read over this question again, and then read over the commandment that the LORD God gave (Gen 2:16b-17). Do you see the difference? When the LORD God gave his commandment, everything was given and only one thing prohibited. With his question, though, the serpent asks the woman if it is true that God forbade everything. The commandment is overwhelmingly positive; the serpent's question casts things in a wholly negative light. We can easily glance one verse ahead to see how the woman responds, but let's stay here a little longer to think about what is taking place.

---

[1] For a more complete account of the creation of man and woman in "original solidarity," see Leonard J. DeLorenzo, *Turn to the Lord: Forming Disciples for Lifelong Conversion* (Collegeville, MN: Liturgical Press, 2021), especially 73–79.

[2] All biblical quotations in this chapter are from the JPS translation, unless otherwise noted.

The question is not honest. An honest question is one where the questioner wants to learn something. This question is dishonest because the serpent is making a proposal with his question. It is a proposal about what this garden really is, and who this God is that commands you. This garden which was created for you, which is filled with gifts for you, in which you yourself have been placed to live—isn't this really more like a prison? Isn't this a place where things are kept from you? And that God, who commanded you, isn't he the one who's holding you down?

The effect of the serpent's question is to make the one who entertains it doubt whether you will be fed.[3] It makes the one who entertains it wonder if this is in fact a god who withholds things, who might potentially threaten your livelihood and continued existence. By accepting the question, human beings waffle over the sheer goodness of the LORD God.

By this point, maybe you've also noticed something else that's a little annoying in this chapter (and the last one). I keep writing "the LORD God" rather than simply "God" when dealing with this twofold account in Genesis chapters 2 and 3. Perhaps you noticed that the serpent did not say "the LORD God" but rather only said "God." For the author of Genesis chapters 2 and 3, the *personal* name of God is YHWH (Yahweh), which is the name God gave to Moses in Exodus 3, a name which Jews would not pronounce. All throughout this narrative, it is the personal name of God that is used, and it is therefore translated as "LORD God." This is the God who draws near, who cares for you, who has mercy on you. This is the one whom you know as *your* God. But the serpent sneaks something in: he subtly denies the personal name of God and says something more like "that God." Suddenly, God is not personal. In fact, this God might be remote, unconcerned with your good, more like a jailer than creator and caretaker. We might not feel much of a difference when we read this in our language, but for a Hebrew-speaking Jew, this is of monumental importance. "God" is suddenly impersonal.

---

[3] See Leon R. Kass, *The Beginning of Wisdom: Reading Genesis* (Chicago: University of Chicago Press, 2006), 83.

The Woman Responds

Having paused over the serpent's question to discern these two massive changes that take place in one seemingly innocuous question, we may now look to the woman's response to see the effect of the serpent's sly proposal. Here is what she says:

> We may eat of the fruit of the other trees of the garden. It is only about the fruit of the tree in the middle of the garden that God said: "You shall not eat of it or touch it, lest you die." (Gen 3:2b-3)

The first part of the woman's response is factually accurate, yet she omits the fact that the fruit of the trees are the produce of the LORD God's generosity. It is like the fruit is just there, rather than all of it being a gift. She does not refer the fruit to the LORD God; the only thing she relates to her Creator is the prohibition: "It is only about the fruit of the tree in the middle of the garden that God said: 'You shall not eat . . .'" To take this one step further, she also fails to recall that this fruit is to be avoided because the LORD God forbade and commanded so; instead, she remembers only that it is to be avoided because of the consequence that might befall them. It is like God is threatening them. She also seems to focus on only one tree in the middle of the garden, missing that there are in fact two in the middle: one for life, and one for knowledge of good and bad (see Gen 2:9). The forbidden thing is the center of her attention, rather than all the many trees that *have* been given, including the one other tree in the middle of the garden that was also given. Finally, what name does she use when referring to her Creator? The name the serpent suggested: "God," not "LORD God" (Yahweh). Subtly—very subtly—this is all a sign of the lack of trust in the LORD God as your Creator and nurturer.[4]

The narrowing of concern to the consequence of disobedience gives the serpent the opening he needs. Did you notice that the woman added something to the commandment that the LORD God gave 'adam? He did not say anything about "touching" the tree, only about

---

[4] Kass, *Beginning of Wisdom*, 84–85; cf. Michael W. Duggan, *The Consuming Fire: A Christian Guide to the Old Testament* (Huntington, IN: Our Sunday Visitor, 2010), 123.

eating the fruit of the tree. Where did that addition come from? Was the man responsible for passing along this commandment to the woman and perhaps did not trust her fully, so he added a little something to the commandment just like parents tell their daughter to "not even touch a cigarette" because they don't want her to smoke one? Or was there some laziness in the act of remembering, like when you have to carry a really important and precise message to someone, and you assume you could never forget it, but you don't rehearse the message in the meantime, which leaves you capable of giving only a somewhat accurate summary rather than the precise message? Either way, many of the ancient Jewish rabbis who commented on this text liked to imagine the serpent now shaking the tree and perhaps the woman drawing near to touch it also.[5] When neither the serpent nor the woman dies from touching it, the concern over the consequence of eating it dissipates. You tell a child to not even touch a cigarette because they will get lung cancer and die, but then they touch one and don't die. If the fear of consequence is the only motivation but the consequences don't line up with the prohibition, the motivation for avoidance weakens.

Taking, Not Receiving

What began as a seemingly innocuous question from the serpent now becomes an outright challenge. The serpent denies that "God" is caring for and protecting you, and claims instead that this "God" is keeping something from you. Should you take this forbidden fruit, you would become like him. You would have knowledge, you would have power, you would have authority. You would make the rules, not him. He is trying to keep you down, so rise up and take what you want. Or, as the serpent puts it:

> You are not going to die, but God knows that as soon as you eat of it your eyes will be opened and you will be like divine beings who know good and bad. (Gen 3:4b-5)

---

[5] See notes to Genesis 3:1b-3 in Adele Berlin and Marc Zvi Brettler, eds., and Michael Fishbane, consulting ed., *The Jewish Study Bible* (Oxford: Oxford University Press, 2004), 16–17.

This is not a lie, per se. Their eyes will be opened, they will know good and bad (by willing and doing what is bad), and they will have made themselves like divine beings who seemingly create themselves and the law at the same time. This is the ultimate temptation: to deny being creatures and presume to be gods.

The woman sizes up the fruit of the tree. She judges that the fruit would be tasty, that it is attractive, and that they can get something out of it.[6] So "she took of its fruit and ate" (3:6). She *takes* it; she does not receive it. And then she turns to her husband, who is right there but has been strangely silent this whole time, and he takes what she gives him. Rather than heed the will of his Creator, he chooses to consummate this act of disobedience and seal their pact to become gods themselves. He chooses to receive from his wife the serpent's poison rather than give to her his trust in the LORD God's goodness.[7]

Everything in this garden was given to them. Everything was there to receive. Only this one thing was forbidden. That one forbidden thing is what they *take*. As soon as they take what they want, they get what they want, though they realize immediately it is not really what they wanted. They *have* acted like gods making their own law, their eyes *are* opened so they can see what they previously did not, they *do* know good and bad because they now have experienced what is bad. The result of it all is that they are ashamed and so they hide themselves, first with fig leaves and then behind the very trees that the LORD God gave to them (3:7-8).

Remember, this all started with the proposal that this garden was not a gift but a prison, and that the LORD God is not personally present to you but rather more like a jailer. By engaging in that way of thinking,

---

[6] These are the three forms of fallen desire known as concupiscence of the flesh, concupiscence of the eyes, and worldly ambition. These desires are present in the three temptations of Christ in the desert (see Luke 4:1-13). They are also explicitly named in First Letter of John: "For all that is in the world, the lust of the flesh and the lust of the eyes and the pride of life, is not of the Father but is of the world" (1 John 2:16). The three evangelical counsels—poverty, chastity, and obedience—are set to curing desire from these corruptions.

[7] One of the most brilliant and probing accounts of the sin of Adam and Eve is the classic account from St. Augustine, who learns to see his own sin in terms of Genesis 3. See Augustine, *The Confessions*, Book II, especially 30–35 (II.4.9–8.16), trans. Maria Boulding (New York: Vintage, 1998).

even just entertaining the possibility that this is how things are, that was the beginning of the Fall. What begins with failing to trust that the Lord God will *give* you what you need, ends with *taking* what you think you want.

What Does God Do?

Man and woman have been stripped of their unadulterated trust in the Lord. They have wounded themselves and each other. They have transformed the good world they were given into a place where they try to hide from the one who created them, who nurtures them, who knows them. Though they deny it, it was their fault. Though *we* deny it, we do the same thing over and over again: it's our fault, our fault, our most grievous fault.

What is even more important than who is at fault, though, is who responds to this tragedy. This account of "the Fall" is as much about what the Lord God does in response as it is about how man and woman will their own destruction. In fact, the Lord God's response is the greater part, though it is not typically considered that way.

What does the Lord God do?

- First, he seeks them. "Where are you?" the Lord God calls out, drawing out his creatures who are hiding from him and from themselves (see 3:9).

- Second, he corrects them. He does not say "Everything is okay" because it's not. They have become less than he has created them and called them to be (see 3:16-19).

- Third, he covers them. They are wounded and vulnerable. They tried to cover up their misdeed and their shame with ill-fitting (and quite itchy!) fig leaves. For them to be seen as they really are would be an unbearable burden. Imagine, for a moment, if all your thoughts were immediately perceptible to everyone else. Until you are healed of your weaknesses and sins and devious thoughts, it is a mercy that we are not transparent to each other. And so the Lord God makes them garments of skin to clothe them (3:21).

- Fourth, he protects them. It may sound strange to suggest that banishing them from the garden is an act of protection, but notice what the Lord God says: "Now that the man has become like one of us, knowing good and bad, what if he should stretch out his hand and take also from the tree of life and eat, and live forever!" (3:22). The problem is not living forever; the problem is living forever *like this*. The Lord God will not allow this sorrow and shame that they have chosen for themselves to go on and on, without end. He removes them from the garden so they don't make it into a living hell.

Even the story of sin is the story of God's mercy. God is the one who responds to sin with mercy. Even when we are not worthy of his care—and especially then—he seeks us, he corrects us, he covers us, he protects us. We must say, "Lord, I am not worthy to receive you" or "Lord, I am not worthy that you should enter under my roof, but only say the word and my soul shall be healed." And the Lord responds by giving us himself. We do not *take* because he gives himself to us. We are rebuilt to *receive* him.

Guiding Your Child to Engage "The Forbidden Fruit"

Overview

A Look from Above
In the previous session we followed the second creation account to see how the LORD God creates human beings, what the garden is like where God places his creature to live, and how the posture for receiving gifts is different from the posture of taking. The difference in those postures will become important here, as the narrative turns to how human beings take rather than receive from our Creator. This particular episode will later connect in a special way to Jesus turning water into wine at Cana, in response to his mother Mary's concern (chapter 8).

A Closer Look
This session is, in a way, a continuation of the one that came before. Now we pay close attention to how, in sin, we as human beings become something other than who God created us to be, how we misuse the world, and how we end up hiding from God.

1st Movement—Welcoming the Word of God

1. Opening Prayer

   Either establish a regular opening prayer or open with a spontaneous and direct prayer to the Lord each time. No matter what, allow the prayer to be personal and simple.

2. Quick Review

   Reviewing the session on Genesis 2 (chapter 1) is important here. Use your child's drawing for the review. Ask your child questions like the ones that follow so that you can review together:

   - How does God create us?
     - By shaping us from the ground and breathing his breath into us.

- What is the garden like where God places human beings?
  - It is filled with trees that God causes to grow and provide us with food.
- How many trees can God's people eat from?
  - All but one. (The one they can't eat from is the tree of the knowledge of good and bad.)
- What is the difference between receiving and taking? Show me with your hands.
  - Openness versus snatching.

2nd Movement—Engaging the Word of God

1. Reading

    Genesis 3:1-10. Read the passage through slowly, out loud.

2. Questions about the Reading

    After you finish reading the passage once, you should read the passage again but this time just one part at a time, as noted below. You will ask your child different questions for different verses of the passage:

    - Read Genesis 3:1 and ask: What is wrong with that question?
      - Pay close attention to the wording. It will be helpful to go back and read together the original commandment in Genesis 2:16-17.
      - Notice how the serpent proposes the *opposite* of what is true about the garden. The serpent asks if God said they can't eat anything from the garden, when in fact the Lord God said they could eat *everything* . . . just not from that one tree.
    - Read Genesis 3:2-3 and ask: What is wrong about the answer to the question?
      - Answer: It is not specific enough. There are *two* trees in the middle of the garden. The woman focuses on only one.

- Note: God never said anything about not *touching* the tree of knowledge of good and bad.
- Read Genesis 3:4-5 and ask: How does the serpent want the woman to treat God?
  - See how the serpent wants her to treat God like someone that is keeping something from you, instead of like someone who created you and gives you everything you need.
- Read Genesis 3:6-7 and ask: What is wrong with what they do? After that, ask: What happens to them?
  - What they do is *take* rather than *receive*.
  - What happens to them is that they are ashamed. Talk about what it means to be ashamed.
- Look together at Genesis 3:8-10, and point out the following:
  - They hide from God. That must be what it is like to be ashamed.
  - But even though they hide from God, God comes looking for them. God wants to find them and be near them.

3. Points to Emphasize

These are some of the main points to emphasize, either as you go along or at the end:

- The serpent wants the people to think the opposite of what is true about God, the garden, and themselves.
- They *take* the fruit they are not supposed to take. They stop *receiving*. Demonstrate the difference with your hands and show again how we receive the Eucharist with open hands (or upon the tongue, of course).
- Even though they are ashamed and hide from God, God wants to find them.

3rd Movement—Reflecting on the Word of God

1. Activity

Draw the scene. Or, if necessary, choose an alternative activity.

2. Discussion

    Ask your child to tell you about the drawing. Ask questions about it. This is a chance for them to teach you.

3. Closing Prayer

    Close with a prayer of thanksgiving for your time together, like the one recommended at the end of the last session.

chapter three

The Passover

(Exod 12:1-20)

Things were not going well for the Israelites in Egypt; in fact, things were getting worse. It had not always been this way. When the whole household of Jacob arrived in Egypt some 430 years earlier, they were welcomed and fed in gratitude for the abundance that Joseph, the beloved son of Jacob, brought upon Egypt. Pharaoh was in Joseph's debt and so Joseph's family was welcomed. That was the beginning of Israel in Egypt. But now, toward the end, the pharaoh who looked favorably upon Israel was long dead, and the new pharaoh "did not know Joseph" (Exod 1:8).[1] He did not remember that the Israelites were a source of his own land's prosperity. When this pharaoh looked upon the Israelites, he saw only a threat to his unrivaled power (see Exod 1:9-10). Indeed, the Israelites had grown very numerous and soon they would be starving: yes, for bread, but even more for liberation from the slavery that this pharaoh forced upon them as he sought to keep them pinned down.

God loved Israel with special affection. This was his people. He considered the nation as a whole to be his "first-born son" (Exod 4:22). When the people cried out from under their bondage, the Lord heard their cry and took notice of them and drew near to raise them out of their misery. Yet the heart of Pharaoh was turned against this people and their God—the heart of Pharaoh obstructed their freedom.

---

[1] All biblical quotations in this chapter come from the JPS translation, unless otherwise noted.

"Who is the LORD that I should heed Him and let Israel go?" Pharaoh cynically questioned. "I do not know the LORD, nor will I let Israel go" (Exod 5:2).

In the events that follow, when things get bad for Pharaoh and his own people cry out to him and his land suffers, he will concede to the Lord's demands and seek relief from this God he denies.[2] But time and again, he reneges on his promises and continues to stiffen his heart against the Israelites.[3] The Lord lets Pharaoh reveal the quality of his own heart.[4] In the end, after Pharaoh repeatedly stiffens his heart, God ratifies Pharaoh's decision and strips him of the freedom to change his mind.

The Lord speaks to Pharaoh through plagues, with Moses as the intermediary. Pharaoh has claimed absolute authority for himself and by turning against the Israelites in hostility, he has denied that this people—the Lord's people—has been a blessing upon his land and kingdom. And so the Lord begins to remove his blessings from the land to reveal to the pharaoh his own dependence on the Lord's absolute power.

If creation itself is secured in the Lord's act of speaking things into existence and giving all things their proper order (see Gen 1), then the plagues may be seen as one measure after another of the Lord removing his act of creation from Egypt. The water that is turned to blood is water Pharaoh takes for granted but that the Lord made into an abode for all the sea creatures. When frogs overrun the land, the proper restriction and balance that holds this chaos at bay is suspended. When gnats emerge from the dust, it is a display of the Lord's power to create life from the earth (see Gen 2:7), yet now that life is not delightful but bothersome. Flies cover the land like a blanket of decay; pestilence strikes the food the Egyptians depend on; boils trouble the integrity of the people's very flesh. Hail comes and the people complain about this evil, which redounds to the good they erstwhile depended on. The locusts that swarm the land devour whatever was saved from the hail. And then darkness covers the land as light, which comes at the dawn of creation (Gen 1:3), is removed.

---

[2] See Exod 8:4, 21, 24; 9:27-28; 10:8-11, 16-17, 24-28.
[3] See Exod 7:13, 14, 22; 8:11, 15, 28; 9:7, 34, 35.
[4] See Exod 7:3-4; 14:4.

Without the Lord's act of creation, everything falls into disorder, chaos, and darkness (cf. Gen 1:2).

Pharaoh's magicians are the first to recognize the supremacy of the Lord's power, for they cannot contend with what the Lord does. Then the Egyptian people recognize the Lord's power as they see how much they depend on what they have taken for granted as the conditions of life, and how helpless they are when those blessings are removed. And yet Pharaoh, though he pleads with Moses at times to beg the Lord to remove the curses upon his land—or, rather, to restore the blessings—only tries to get what he wants. He will not yield himself to the Lord, as he goes right back to imposing his own will as soon as what troubled him or his people or his land is restored to its previous order. And so the Lord speaks to Pharaoh through one last plague—the most terrible of the ten.

The final blessing and act of creation to be removed from the land of Egypt and its people will be the gift and blessing of life itself:

> [E]very first-born in the land of Egypt shall die, from the first-born of Pharaoh who sits on his throne to the first-born of the slave girl who is behind the millstones; and all the first-born of the cattle. And there shall be a loud cry in all the land of Egypt, such as has never been or will ever be again; but not a dog shall snarl at any of the Israelites, at man or beast—in order that you may know that the LORD makes a distinction between Egypt and Israel. (Exod 11:5-7)

The Lord makes a distinction indeed, for Israel is *his* first-born and the tenth plague is the sign of his love for his first-born, illuminated against the dark backdrop of Pharaoh's hardness of heart.

The Lamb

It is the blood of the lamb that marks God's people. When life is removed from the first-born in Egypt, the lamb's blood on the doorposts and lintel of each house not only preserves the life of the first-born of the Israelites but indicates that these are the households of the people the Lord claims as his own. The blood of the lamb delivers them from death and the flesh of the lamb forms them as one people.

While this plague, like the others, is one occasion of the Lord speaking to Pharaoh to let his people go, even more than the others it is characterized by an act of extraordinary favor and blessing upon the Lord's own people. As the Lord makes his power known to Pharaoh, he also makes his mercy known to Israel. The Lord will now show the Israelites that he is the one who saves them (see, later, Exod 15:1-3).

The Lord thus instructs his people to take one lamb for every household, from which both the blood and the flesh will be necessary. For that entire household, the blood will surround the doorway to preserve this family, while the flesh will be the meal that feeds them all, as one family. It is a meal prepared intentionally, according to the Lord's instructions, so that the preparation itself is an act of obedience to and trust in the Lord who speaks to his people and will soon act on their behalf. The blood, therefore, will be the people's pledge of confidence in the Lord, who, when "[he] goes through to smite the Egyptians, . . . will see the blood on the lintel and the two doorposts, and . . . will pass over the door and not let the Destroyer enter and smite your home" (Exod 12:23). The flesh, then, that is consumed inside the household, not only strengthens and nourishes the people, but also brings the entire household together as one, and brings the entire people who observe this ritual—from household to household—together as one people. For God loves all of Israel as one child, his "first-born."

The Bread

The Passover is enacted so that the Israelites may be free of the Egyptians. Israel cannot worship the Lord freely and wholly while slaves in Egypt, and so the Lord has come to deliver them from slavery to freedom. The whole point is that the Israelites leave Egypt: freed from captivity to Pharaoh, freed for worship of the Lord.

The Israelites are a people called to move, to journey. The moment Pharaoh and the Egyptians seek to drive them out of the land, they are to move without delay. They are a people preparing to take flight. And so, alongside the feast of the paschal lamb, the Israelites are to prepare and eat "unleavened bread." This is bread that is made in haste, without the luxury of the time needed to allow the dough to rise. It is flatbread.[5] This bread is both the sign and the sustenance of a people

---

[5] See Robert Alter's translation of *matsot* as flatbread, with his compelling explanatory note to Exodus 12:8 in *The Five Books of Moses: A Translation with Commentary* (New York: W. W. Norton, 2004), 377.

on their way, hastening toward the fulfillment of a promise. This is bread of a people not at home where they are but moving toward their true homeland.

Indeed, as soon as "the Egyptians urged the people on, impatient to have them leave the country, . . . the people took their dough before it was leavened" (Exod 12:33-34). Just like the lamb, the bread is both sustenance for the people and a sign of the people's trust in the Lord. By heeding the command to leave their bread unleavened, they wait with expectation for the Lord to do for them what he has promised to do. We might even say that the *lack* of leaven is the expression of the Israelites' nascent faith and hope in the Lord. This is the faith and hope that will rise into worship when this people is finally and ultimately free.

Salvation and the Journey

The Passover is both gift and promise: that which is done and that which is yet to come. With the blood of the lamb, we see the mercy of the Lord upon his people, who are preserved and delivered from death on this one night. With the flesh of the lamb, we see the people formed as one—household by household—as both the reality and the image of what they truly are and are to become: God's one people. And with the unleavened bread, we see already the road ahead: this is traveling food for a people called into the fulfilment of the Lord's promises.

There is an act of salvation at the Passover; there is also a pledge of future glory. The Israelites are commanded to make this day into "one of remembrance: . . . [to] celebrate it as a festival to the LORD throughout the ages; . . . as an institution for all time" (Exod 12:14). The great act of deliverance is never to be forgotten, for it is the source of the people's freedom, the price the Lord paid to ransom his beloved from slavery. And yet, so long as this is a people who still journeys toward the fullness of the Lord's presence, this perpetual institution is also the feast of ongoing departure, of flight to the promised land of freedom. The paschal lamb and the unleavened bread make present and signify the already and the not yet.

Guiding Your Child to Engage "The Passover"

Overview

A Look from Above

The previous two sessions focused on the account of creation and the fall from Genesis chapters 2 and 3. This session takes us to the Book of Exodus, from which the episodes for this session and the next come. In fact, our episodes from the Old Testament come in three pairs. The first pair (chapters 1 and 2) is from the Book of Genesis, the middle pair (chapters 3 and 4) is from the Book of Exodus, and the final pair (chapters 5 and 6) is from the two books of Kings. It is easier to track the connections within each pair, and it takes a little more work to make connections across pairs. Therefore, we will be sure to take time remembering what we did in prior sessions before moving on to the passage in each new session. This particular episode will later connect most especially to the Last Supper (chapter 10).

A Closer Look

This session brings us to Egypt, where the Israelites are enslaved. We are approaching the great event of the exodus, when, through Moses, God leads his people out of slavery. The particular event we focus on here is the Passover, which comes on the occasion of the tenth and final plague—the one that forces Pharaoh to drive Israel out of his land. We will pay attention to the sacrifice and meal the Israelites are told to prepare, which concerns the paschal lamb and the unleavened bread.

1st *Movement—Welcoming the Word of God*

1. Opening Prayer

    By now, hopefully you have established a good routine for this opening prayer.

2. Quick Review

    Reviewing Genesis chapters 2 and 3 (the first two sessions) is helpful here. Ask your child to do the following, using the drawings they created if possible:

- Tell you about the garden where God placed human beings.
- Tell you about the difference between receiving and taking.
- Tell you what the man and woman did because they were ashamed.
- Tell you what God did when the man and woman were hiding. (Notice how God coming to his people is a consistent theme all throughout Scripture. God comes to his people here, too, as they are in slavery in Egypt. God always makes the first move.)

2nd Movement—Engaging the Word of God

1. Set the Scene (since the scene has changed)

    Some key points to help orient your child:

    - God's people, Israel, all go to Egypt. (If your child is familiar with the Joseph story from the end of Genesis, you can use that to place this in context.)
    - Four hundred years later, the ruler of Egypt—Pharaoh—sees the Israelites as enemies and forces them into slavery. The people are miserable. Their lives are terrible. They are not free.
    - God hears the cries of his people and comes to them to set them free, calling Moses to help lead the people to freedom. But Pharaoh will not let the people go. So God sends ten plagues to Egypt to make Pharaoh want to set the people free, but Pharaoh is stubborn. It isn't until the last plague that Pharaoh finally gives in.

2. Reading

    Exodus 12:1-20. Read the passage through slowly, out loud.

3. Discussing the Reading

    There are some difficult things for a child to understand in this reading. We need to spend time with children here to help them grow in understanding. You might choose to pull from what is provided earlier in this chapter, or else talk about things like these:

    - God loves Israel like his only child. Pharaoh is keeping Israel in slavery. God is acting to free his people from slavery.

- Pharaoh is very, very stubborn. He wants to be in charge. The plagues are sent to convince Pharaoh to change his mind. He still won't let the people go.

- The last plague is the death of the firstborn. All throughout Egypt, the firstborn child will die on the same night, whether humans or animals. This is the most terrible plague, but Pharaoh has ignored everything else. God will protect his people from this plague and he tells them what they must do. That is where this Passover meal comes in. The death of the firstborn will "pass over" Israel, and then they will "pass over" from slavery to freedom.

4. Questions about the Reading

The main focus here is on the meal. These questions help your child to set their attention on this meal:

- What food is talked about in this passage?
    - Note that there are two foods: lamb and bread.
- What is the lamb used for?
    - First, the blood of the lamb is placed on the doorposts of each house. This will protect the people from death.
    - Next, the whole lamb is cooked and eaten. This is the main meal for the people.
    - Last, God tells the people to prepare this meal and celebrate this feast every year from now on, to remember what God has done for them.
    - Note: when we call Jesus "Lamb of God," we are comparing Jesus to this Passover lamb.
- What is different about this bread?
    - Really emphasize that this is *unleavened* bread. That means that it is bread that is made quickly and not given time to rise, with leaven. This is bread for a people that is getting ready for a journey.
    - Note: the bread that is consecrated at Mass is always *unleavened* bread.

5. Points to Emphasize

   These are some of the main points to emphasize, either as you go along or at the end:

   - God loves his people like his only child and frees them from slavery.
   - The blood of the lamb protects the people from death.
   - The main meal at Passover is the lamb whose blood saves them.
   - The bread that is prepared is *unleavened* because it is made quickly as food for the journey.

3rd Movement—Reflecting on the Word of God

1. Activity

   Draw the scene. Or, if necessary, choose an alternative activity.

2. Discussion

   Ask your child to tell you about the drawing. Ask questions about it. This is a chance for them to teach you.

3. Closing Prayer

   Close with a prayer of thanksgiving for your time together, like the one recommended at the end of the first session.

chapter four

The Manna

(Exod 16:1-35)

Everyone enjoys being free. Well, maybe not. It might be more accurate to say that everyone enjoys the *idea* of being free—especially their *own* idea of being free. What happens when freedom is not what you thought it would be? What if it turns out that you enjoy the meager comforts of your captivity more than you enjoy not being bossed around? What could make you wish that things would just go back to the way they were, when you were unfree? Hunger could make you wish that.

Through the plagues and by the Passover, the Lord delivered his people from slavery in Egypt. They passed through the Red Sea, where their pursuers were taken away from them forever. On the other side of that sea, they are totally free—not only are they out of the land of their captivity, they are also free from the threat of their captors recapturing them. But standing there, on the other side of the sea—free at last in the desert—the Israelites soon start doing a very strange thing. They begin wishing they were back in Egypt, because they're hungry.

Something has changed within them. Not long before, the whole people had erupted into songs of praise, thanking the Lord for taking them out of Egypt (Exod 15:1-20). In a month's time, they have gone from rejoicing and praising to complaining and blaming. "The Israelites said to [Moses and Aaron], 'If only we had died by the hand of the LORD in the land of Egypt, when we sat by the fleshpots, when we ate our fill of bread! For you have brought us out into this wilderness to starve this whole congregation to death" (Exod 16:3).[1] It is as if parents have taken their children to a park but—God forbid!—forgot to pack snacks. As every parent knows, there shall be no peace in that place.

To be fair, the Israelites are hungry. It is likely that the unleavened bread they took with them when they left Egypt is all but exhausted. The desert is not a supple place, certainly not bountiful enough to provide food for an entire people. It is not hard to grasp the Israelites' fear and frustration. Hunger does things to you.

We might even empathize with the Israelites, recognizing that we too would likely wish to be back in the place that provided for our needs. At first it might be hard to imagine that they would want to be back "in the land of Egypt," but if it is a choice between death in Egypt with full stomachs and death in the desert with empty ones, maybe Egypt isn't such a bad option, all things considered.

That way of thinking seems reasonable until we realize the choice they are really making. Faced with hardship and the raw pain of their own basic needs, the Israelites turn their hearts back to the place and the people that abused them. They long for that perverse protection rather than turning to the Lord who heard their cries when they were in slavery and took them by the hand to lead them out of that misery. The Lord preserved their life by the blood of the lamb, fed their families with lamb's flesh, and prepared them for their journey by instructing them to pack up the unleavened bread. The memory of the Lord's care for them has faded quickly. They do not call out to the Lord to feed them; instead, they pine for the conditions of slavery in Egypt.

Nevertheless, the Lord feeds them.

Why the Lord Feeds, and How

The people are hungry; the Lord feeds them. If you were to ask why the Lord feeds them, the answer appears self-evident: he feeds them *because* they are hungry. While this is not untrue, it is also not the whole truth. In fact, it may not even be the primary reason why the Lord acts as he does. Listen to what the Lord first says to Moses after the people murmur, grumble, and complain about their hunger and

---

[1] All biblical quotations in this chapter come from the JPS translation, unless otherwise noted.

the undesirable conditions of their newfound freedom: "I will rain down bread for you from the sky, and the people shall go out and gather each day that day's portion—that I may thus test them, to see whether they follow My instructions or not" (Exod 16:4).

Certainly, the Lord gives what he gives so that his people will not be hungry, but even more, he gives what he gives to see whether or not they trust him. There is something more than food at stake here. This is about whom the people trust to provide for all their needs, each day. Up to this moment, they have shown themselves more trusting of the Egyptians than God their liberator. Will they learn to trust the Lord, first and foremost?

What does the Lord give them? Honestly, they don't know: "When the Israelites saw it, they said to one another, 'What is it?'—for they did not know what it was" (Exod 16:15). Moses has to tell them, "That is the bread which the LORD has given you to eat" (Exod 16:16). This is utterly important: this is not merely bread; it is *bread given to you by the Lord*. The word "manna," by which the bread comes to be known, translates as "what is it?" The question of what this bread is never gets fully settled. To recognize this bread for what it is, each and every one must confess that "this is the bread the Lord gives to *me*, to *us*." The bread itself is a gift—to receive it means to receive a gift.

How do you receive a gift as a gift? By trusting the one who gives it to you and being grateful in response. The Lord knows his people. He knows they have fickle hearts. He knows they are quick to forget what he has done for them. And so with the food he gives them in the desert he will teach them to listen to him, to follow him, to trust him.

Each morning the Lord will give his people "bread from the sky"—bread from heaven—but there are three conditions the people must heed in order to receive and benefit from this bread, the manna.

- First, they must only gather what they need and not try to store more. Whatever they try to store will rot.

- Second, they must gather this bread daily. This is their *daily* bread. They gather for that day and not for tomorrow. In heeding these first two conditions, they must thus trust that the Lord will provide for them again *tomorrow*. Take only what you need for today and trust that the Lord will give you tomorrow what you need for tomorrow.

- The third and final condition, then, is that on one particular day, they do what they do not do on the other days: they take double. That is because for one day of the week—the Sabbath—no bread will be given. That day is a day of rest: a day of rest for the Lord, and he shares his rest with his people. To sustain them on that day, then, the Lord will provide double on the day before the Sabbath. The people must gather double in preparation for the Sabbath, and when they store the bread overnight then, it will not rot. Should the people go out to gather bread on the Sabbath, their labors will be in vain, for there shall be no manna anywhere.

By giving this bread from heaven, the Lord is feeding his hungry people. By implementing these specific conditions, the Lord is forming the people to trust him, each day and for tomorrow. By giving the people a Sabbath, the Lord is sharing the joy of rest with them—they are not bound to their labors; rather, they get to taste the fruits of freedom. The gift and conditions of manna form an education in trust, a pedagogy for clinging to the Lord, healing those wounded by slavery and sin, teaching them how to welcome the Lord.

The manna is the main focus of Exodus 16, but there is also another food the Lord provides for his people. While the manna appears in the morning, quail appear for them each night. They are thus given both bread and meat to eat, which is reminiscent of their Passover meal when they feasted on the meat of the lamb and unleavened bread. As they receive this food from the Lord's hand for their forty years of journeying through the desert, the food of every morning and evening is a reminder of the great act of liberation the Lord is working for his people: out of slavery in Egypt, into freedom in the Promised Land. They are eating not just food, but the Lord's goodness day by day.

Guiding Your Child to Engage "The Manna"

Overview

A Look from Above

In the last session, we gave our attention to the Passover, where the lamb and the unleavened bread were the focus of the meal. By the blood of the lamb, God protected his people from death, to lead them out of slavery toward freedom. The unleavened bread was food for them as a people in flight. In the episode of this session, then, we join the Israelites out in the wilderness, likely when that bread ran out. Between the last episode and this one, we find two ways in which the Lord feeds his people on the journey from Egypt to the Promised Land. This particular episode will later connect most especially with the Bread of Life discourse (chapter 9).

A Closer Look

We join the Israelites on the other side of the Red Sea where, one month after God's marvelous deed liberating them from slavery, the people complain about hunger and wish to return to slavery. The centerpiece of this episode is the food the Lord provides—"manna" along with quail—but this food is not just food. It is also and primarily a test of and an education in the people's trust in the Lord. The conditions for receiving the manna are therefore crucial.

1st Movement—Welcoming the Word of God

1. Opening Prayer

2. Quick Review

    Reviewing Exodus 12 (the Passover) is helpful since that places today's episode in context. Use your child's drawing for review, if possible. Here are some key points you might consider sharing (or putting into question form) to have your child try to recall and tell you about the Passover:

    • God came to save his people, Israel, from Egypt and Pharaoh.

The Manna 49

- The last plague was the death of the firstborn and God saved his people from this plague (by the blood of lamb on their doors).
- The Passover meal centered around a whole lamb for each household.
- They prepared and ate unleavened bread because it was bread made quickly for people setting out immediately on a journey.

2nd *Movement—Engaging the Word of God*

1. Set the Scene (since the scene has changed)

    There is one key point for setting the scene:

    - God's people, Israel, have now been freed from Egypt and they are out in the desert. It is about one month after they left Egypt.

2. Reading

    Exodus 16:1-35. Read the passage through slowly, out loud.

3. Learning More about the Reading

    After reading the narrative through once, we now want to go back to understand the important elements of this episode better. This may be done through asking questions and then, as needed, going back to read different parts of the text:

    - What are the people like and what are they doing at the beginning of this story? (See 16:2-3.)
        - They are hungry.
        - They are complaining to Moses and Aaron, and thus to God.
        - They even wish they were back in Egypt because at least there they had food. They want to be back in slavery rather than free with God!
    - What does God say that he will give them? (See 16:4.)
        - God promises "bread from heaven" (or "bread from the sky").
        - Your child might also note the quail that God gives in the evening, but if not, there is no need to mention that yet.

- What does God say that the people must do to receive this bread? There are three things. (See 16:4-5, 19-20, 22-26.)
  - First, they must gather this bread each day.
  - Second, they cannot store it overnight. They can only take what they need for one day at a time.
  - Third, they cannot gather on the seventh day, which is the Sabbath or the day of rest with the Lord. Instead, they will gather twice as much the day before, and that night only can they store it.
  - Ask your child something like: Do you see how they have to trust God to feed them each day?
- What is this bread called? (See 16:31, and then 16:15-16.)
  - The Israelites called this bread "manna" (16:31).
  - Earlier they said "What is it?" (16:15). Manna actually means "what is it?" in Hebrew. So the name of the bread is literally "What is it?"
  - Moses answers the question "What is it?" for them: "That is the bread the Lord has given you to eat" (16:5). The most important thing is that they know this is what God gives them, that God is the one feeding them.
- Does God give them anything else to eat? (See 16:12-13.)
  - God gives them manna in the morning and then gives them quail to eat at night.
  - God provides food for them, day and night.

4. Points to Emphasize

These are some of the main points to emphasize, either as you go along or at the end:

- The manna is bread God gives his people from heaven.
- The people have to trust God to give them this food every day—they cannot store it and they need to gather twice as much on the sixth day so they can rest on the Sabbath.

The Manna 51

- Manna means "What is it?" The answer is that it is the bread God gives them.
- At Passover, they ate meat (lamb) and unleavened bread. In the desert, God feeds them in a similar way: meat (quail) at night and manna (bread) in the morning.
- The point is to trust the Lord to feed you. God feeds them this way for forty years.

3rd *Movement—Reflecting on the Word of God*

1. Activity

   Draw the scene. Or, if necessary, choose an alternative activity.

2. Discussion

   Ask your child to tell you about the drawing.

3. Closing Prayer

chapter five

The Prophet's Strength

(1 Kgs 19:1-21)

The prophet Elijah had a very good day at work, which then turned into a very bad day. Living in the ninth century BC, Elijah was a fiery reformer during the reign of the indecisive and fickle King Ahab of the northern kingdom of Israel. Ahab was under the control of his wife, Jezebel, who was the daughter of the king of Sidon. Through Ahab, Jezebel led the Israelites to abandon their God and worship instead the Canaanite god of storm and fertility, Baal.[1] God's own people had turned their hearts away from him, chasing instead the spectacles of power and might. Elijah was charged with calling the people back. His most magnificent work took place on a mountain top, where his greatest success led him into the greatest danger.

The Power atop Carmel

Since the Israelites had come to worship Baal, trusting this false god to bring them water and fertility, Elijah proclaimed a three-year drought over the land to show the people that the LORD God, not Baal, ruled the land and the crops. As the drought intensified, Ahab and especially Jezebel became more and more enraged, and the people became ever more desperate. Jezebel had been killing off prophets in

---

[1] A helpful and succinct introduction to Elijah, Ahab, and Jezebel is provided in Michael W. Duggan, *The Consuming Fire: A Christian Guide to the Old Testament* (Huntington, IN: Our Sunday Visitor, 2010), 253–54.

retribution, so that eventually only Elijah was working on the Lord God's behalf in public. Elijah resolved to reveal once and for all the true authority of the Lord God and the futility of the foreign gods. So Elijah went to Ahab and instructed him to summon the people of Israel and 450 prophets of Baal, to come meet him atop Mount Carmel.

Upon Mount Carmel, Elijah stages a showdown. The purpose is to show the Israelites which God is true, which one holds the power of rain and life in his hands, which one deserves their fidelity and trust. Before the eyes of the people, the prophets of Baal will prepare one bull for sacrifice, and the prophet Elijah will prepare another. They will each lay their bull out on wood but they will not set the wood ablaze. Instead, the prophets of Baal will pray to their god to light the wood and consume their sacrifice, and Elijah will pray to the Lord God to do the same. The people agree that "the god who responds with fire, that one is God" (1 Kgs 18:24).[2]

The prophets of Baal go first. They spend the entire day calling upon their god. They dance and they chant. They "gashed themselves with knives and spears, according to their practice, until the blood streamed over them" (1 Kgs 18:28). They whipped themselves into a frenzy. Noon passed. Then the late afternoon hours passed. Nothing happened. Their god was silent.

After the prophets of Baal had exhausted themselves, Elijah drew the people of Israel close to him. He took twelve stones to represent the twelve tribes of Israel, and arranged the stones into an altar. He laid the bull upon the altar and he built a trench around the altar. Then he poured huge jars of water all over the bull—three times he did this. The water soaked the bull and filled the trench around the altar. Having now made ignition all the more unlikely, Elijah began praying to the Lord God, begging him to call the people back to himself through his mighty work. And with that, the Lord God sent fire upon the altar and consumed the sacrifice. In response, the people cried out, "The Lord alone is God, the Lord alone is God!" (1 Kgs 18:39). Elijah then slayed the 450 prophets of Baal, releasing the people from their deceptive deeds.

---

[2] All biblical quotations in this chapter come from the JPS translation, unless otherwise noted.

That was a very good day at work for the prophet Elijah. But no sooner did word of his deed reach Queen Jezebel's ears, than she put out a death warrant for the prophet Elijah. The entire kingdom under her command would be unleashed upon Elijah, to bring him to ruin. So great was Elijah's deed on behalf of the LORD God that the greatest storm of fury arose in Jezebel, and that storm was unleashed in Elijah's direction.

Elijah fled. He ran for his life. He ran for five days straight down south, away from Jezebel's palace. Then he ran for another full day out east into the wilderness. Weak, dejected, and afraid, Elijah sat down under a broom tree and begged the Lord to take his life. Less than a week after performing his greatest deed, Elijah had lost the will to live.

The Bread from the Angel

Elijah asked for death, but the Lord gave him new life. While Elijah slept under the broom tree—weighed down by his misery—the Lord sent an angel to him, to bring him food and drink. The angel instructed the prophet to "Arise and eat" (1 Kgs 19:5). What Elijah found was a cake baked on hot stones, and a jar of water. So he ate, then he returned to his sleep.

The angel of the Lord did not bring nourishment to Elijah so that the prophet might sleep more contentedly. The Lord intended something else entirely for his prophet, whom the angel approached in his weary state. Waking Elijah again, the angel repeated the command but this time added to it: "Arise and eat, or the journey will be too much for you" (1 Kgs 19:7). Filling his belly and slaking his thirst was not all the prophet was meant to do. Indeed, the Lord intended a journey for his prophet—a long and arduous journey, deep into the desert. The food the angel provided strengthened Elijah to walk for forty days and forty nights, traveling somewhere between six hundred and one thousand miles.[3] This man who had collapsed in sorrow and begged for death was filled with the strength to walk for nearly six full weeks, because the Lord fed him.

---

[3] Adele Berlin and Marc Zvi Brettler, eds., and Michael Fishbane, consulting ed., *The Jewish Study Bible* (Oxford: Oxford University Press, 2004), 717, note to 19:8.

At the end of Elijah's journey, he arrived at another mountain—Horeb—where a different journey would begin.[4]

The Silence of Presence and the Renewal of Mission

By the time Elijah arrived at Mount Horeb, he had done quite a bit of traveling. He had fled five days south from Mount Carmel to get away from Jezebel. Then he ran a full day into the desert to get away from everyone and anyone, out of civilization, into seclusion—that's where he prayed for death. After being strengthened by the food from the angel's hand, Elijah then walked for forty days and forty nights, deeper and deeper into the desert wilderness.

When he stood on Mount Carmel, he was the only prophet of God present, but he was full of confidence and passion. Now, at Mount Horeb, he is still alone, but his temperament has changed. As he confesses aloud to the Lord God: "I am moved by zeal for the Lord, the God of Hosts, for the Israelites have forsaken Your covenant, torn down Your altars, and put Your prophets to the sword. I alone am left, and they are out to take my life" (1 Kgs 19:10; 19:14). His passion for the Lord is now conditioned by his fear of his persecutors; it even seems that he has forgotten the great deed he effected at Mount Carmel and the people's resounding response.

It is worth remembering that it was a god of the storm that Elijah had opposed, a god of fire that the false prophets called for and the people wanted to see, and a god who would shake with fear the land that Queen Jezebel served. Now that Elijah stands alone at Horeb, he will meet his God, but not in the storm, the fire, or the earthquake. It is not Baal who waits for him and comes to meet him; it is not Baal who strengthened him under the broom tree; not Baal who calls him and will send him. It is the Lord God of Israel who comes to his prophet Elijah in "a still, small voice" (1 Kgs 19:12).[5]

---

[4] Horeb is often identified with Sinai, where the Lord met Moses. See, for example, Israel W. Slotki, *Kings*, ed. A. Cohen, Soncino Books of the Bible (London: Soncino, 1968), 138; and Norman Snaith's exegesis of 1 Kings in *The Interpreter's Bible*, vol. 3, *Kings; Chronicles; Ezra; Nehemiah; Esther; Job*, ed. Nolan Harmon (New York: Abingdon, 1954), 162.

[5] The translation provided here is the alternate translation in Berlin and Brettler, *The Jewish Study Bible*, 717. The primary translation in the JPS is "a soft murmuring

The deepest journey that Elijah makes is the journey to receive his LORD God in silence. Elijah receives him; he hears him; he knows him. We might think that if and when the Lord comes to us, his presence will be undeniable and recognizing him will be obvious. But Elijah shows us something else. Elijah exercised the wisdom and wherewithal to separate from the spectacles of the wind, earthquake, and fire. He did not identify brute displays of might with the God of Israel. Yes, it was the LORD God rather than Baal who was revealed as true by the fire on Mount Carmel, but those who based their fidelity on such displays were subject to being deceived by counterfeit displays in the future. Those who only seek gods of might will often be seduced by the mighty. Instead of being seduced, Elijah waited on the Lord as the one who would speak to his soul.[6] The food the Lord gave Elijah by the hand of the angel strengthened this weary prophet to seek the Lord in silence, which outlasts every storm.

The most peculiar part of this entire episode is that as soon as Elijah meets the Lord in this deep intimacy upon the mountain, after having traveled hundreds of miles over the span of many weeks, the Lord immediately says to Elijah, "Go back" (1 Kgs 19:15). Elijah has gone to great lengths to put distance between himself and Jezebel's troops, and he has gone to even greater lengths to seek the Lord in the silence of this most remote place, but nevertheless the Lord commands him to go back. The man who goes back does not go back unchanged. When Elijah fled to the desert, he was alone—"I alone am left," he cried twice to the Lord (19:10, 14). As he goes back, though, he goes having encountered the Lord's presence and he now moves in obedience to the Lord's command. Fed first by bread from the angel and ultimately by the presence of the Lord, Elijah now consumes the Lord's words and turns in haste to do the Lord's work.

---

sound." Other translations include "a light murmuring sound" (NJB), "a tiny whispering sound" (NAB), and "a sound of a gentle stillness" (ASV, which is the most literal Hebrew translation).

[6] Ronald S. Wallace makes this point nicely in *Elijah and Elisha: Expositions from the Book of Kings* (Edinburgh: Oliver and Boyd, 1957), 48.

Guiding Your Child to Engage "The Prophet's Strength"

Overview

A Look from Above

This session begins the third of the three pairs of episodes from the Old Testament. The first pair came from the Book of Genesis, the second from the Book of Exodus, and the third now comes from the books of 1 and 2 Kings. Whereas the scenes from Genesis had to do with the creation of human beings and those from Exodus featured God's people Israel, these scenes from 1 and 2 Kings concern two of the prophets of Israel: Elijah and his successor Elisha. The time and setting for this pair of episodes are different, but God's action is the same: he feeds his people. This particular episode will later connect most especially with the encounter in Emmaus (chapter 11).

A Closer Look

The prophet Elijah lives and serves in a time of great hardship and infidelity in Israel. This is well after the exodus from Egypt and the entrance of Israel into the Promised Land. Setting up the scene a little bit is important, though we will not feel the need to provide a full-blown historical account between the Book of Exodus and 1 Kings. Here we encounter the prophet who does great deeds in service to the Lord for the people of Israel, but is thereby exhausted, made fearful, and turned desperate. What takes place is an event of renewal and rebirth, where the Lord strengthens the servant he calls.

1st Movement—Welcoming the Word of God

1. Opening Prayer

2. Quick Review

    It is good to review both Exodus 12 and 16 here (the Passover and the manna). It is best, if possible, to ask your child to look at his or her drawings from those sessions to help the two of you remember what they were all about. Using the drawings from previous sessions is from now on a "best practice." A few quick points are key for this review.

- In both the Passover and with the manna in the desert, God feeds his people for their journey.
- After the scene with the manna, Israel wanders in the desert for forty years, but the Lord continues to provide them with daily bread.
- The point in both events is to trust the Lord to feed you and save you.

2nd Movement—Engaging the Word of God

1. Set the Scene

   Since we are only reading 1 Kings 19 for this session, it is important to help set the scene for your child on the basis of what comes immediately before, that is, 1 Kings 18. See the opening of this chapter for a narrative summary. The key points are these:

   - Elijah is one of God's great prophets in Israel. As a prophet, he speaks God's word and does God's works in Israel, especially to guide the people back to God when they stray.
   - In a showdown, Elijah has just defeated 450(!) prophets of a false god. Those false prophets were trying to lead the people away from the true God. Elijah, who was by himself, beat all of them with God's help.
   - But because Elijah was so successful, the queen who was ruling Israel at that time and hated God wanted to kill Elijah and therefore sent her whole army after him. So Elijah ran away, fearing for his life.

2. Reading in Parts, with Questions

   Since this is a longer passage, you might consider reading it in parts, with questions and discussion mixed in (rather than reading the whole thing through). If you like that idea, the following sections and questions may guide you.

- Read 1 Kings 19:1-4 and ask: The whole army is after Elijah—so how does Elijah feel?
    - At the very least, recognize that Elijah is *very* afraid.
    - At your discretion, perhaps help your child to see that Elijah is so afraid and desperate that he actually asks to die (v. 4).
- Read 1 Kings 19:5-9a and ask: Who comes to Elijah when he is afraid and by himself, and what does Elijah receive?
    - Note that an angel comes to Elijah. It is important to stress that angels are God's messengers. The angel is therefore sent by God.
    - See that Elijah receives bread (a cake) and water from the angel. In fact, he receives these things twice. Note that he is in the desert, alone. These are not things that would be there otherwise.
    - Recognize what happens to Elijah when he eats and drinks: he receives strength and then he journeys very, very far.
    - You might note that what Elijah eats is the bread of angels.
- Read 1 Kings 19:9b-14 and ask: When Elijah gets to the mountain he was journeying to, how does he meet the Lord?
    - This can be a little tricky because he speaks to the Lord right from the start. As best you can, help your child to see that Elijah *knows* the Lord's presence fully in the silence (19:12-13).
    - Notice that Elijah traveled very, very far with the strength the bread from the angel gave him to be with the Lord in silence.
- Read 1 Kings 19:15 and ask: What does God tell Elijah to do right after Elijah met God in the silence?
    - See that God tells Elijah to "go back." This means Elijah is going back to where he ran away from. He was afraid, now he will be brave.
    - Point out that God gives Elijah a mission. Elijah's meeting with the Lord gave him strength and purpose.

3. Points to Emphasize

   These are some of the main points to emphasize, either as you go along or at the end:

   - Elijah started off afraid, tired, and very sad. God sent his angel to give Elijah food and drink so that he could have new strength for his journey.
   - The end of Elijah's long journey was meeting the Lord in silence. The Lord "speaks" to Elijah's heart.
   - Elijah receives a new mission from the Lord and the courage to take on that mission.
   - Takeaway: God strengthens the servant he calls.

3rd Movement—Reflecting on the Word of God

1. Activity

   Draw the scene.

2. Discussion

   Ask your child to tell you about the drawing.

3. Closing Prayer

chapter six

The Abundant Bread

(2 Kgs 4:42-44)

It is easy to see something small and dismiss it as insignificant. This is indeed a small passage. It comes at the end of a chapter, following three comparatively longer passages, each of which seems more spectacular than this last one.

The first story in this cycle tells of how the prophet helped lift a widowed woman out of poverty (2 Kgs 4:1-7); the second recounts how a childless woman bears a son after the prophet's foretelling, how that son dies, how he is then brought back to life (4:8-37); and the third speaks of how the prophet neutralizes poison in a stew given to his disciples (4:38-41). When we get to the final and shortest passage in this cycle, it does not quite match the drama: a man brings bread that does not seem to be enough for the hungry people, but it turns out to be more than enough. While this is good news for the hungry people, there is no overcoming of poverty, no unexpected births and raisings, no protection against poison. And yet this short and seemingly simple narrative reveals something profound about the goodness of the Lord and those who are to benefit from his goodness.

The Offering

A man comes to the prophet Elisha and offers him the first fruits of the harvest. This offering is what gets everything going. The first fruits are normally reserved for God and the Levitical priests, who lead the people in worship. Since the northern kingdom of Israel was at that time in a state of infidelity to God—still following foreign gods as it did in the time of Elijah—it would seem that this man brings the first fruits to Elijah's successor, Elisha, because he considered him the true servant of the true religion in Israel.[1] Yet, even though these are the first fruits of the harvest, this is still a humble offering. Each of the twenty loaves of barley bread is like a small biscuit, or a penny roll.[2] For a person to eat one of these would amount to nothing more than a light snack, certainly nowhere near a full meal, let alone a daily portion. When the man gives these twenty loaves to Elisha, the prophet is surrounded by a hundred people who are all starving in the midst of a famine. Clearly, the unanticipated offering is insufficient for the great hunger all around Elisha.

We may think we know this story, or at least one like it. Lots of people and not enough bread, so the miracle-worker must end up multiplying the bread. But this is where our memory of the deeds of Jesus in the gospels can lead us to assume the wrong thing about an event in the Old Testament. As we will later see (in coming chapters), there is an important connection between this episode in 2 Kings and what Jesus does in his own time, but if we are too quick to assume that Elisha once did exactly what Jesus later does, we blind ourselves to what actually takes place here.

The Action

What does Elisha do? First, upon receiving this offering, he immediately orders his attendant to give it to the people. Elisha is surrounded by hungry people, he has received bread, and so with haste he transitions from receiving to giving. When his attendant protests that there is clearly not enough bread for the many hungry mouths, Elisha persists: "Give it to the people and let them eat" (2 Kgs 4:43a, JPS). Though

---

[1] H. J. Austel and R. D. Patterson, "2 Kings," in *Expositor's Bible Commentary: Old Testament*, ed. Kenneth L. Barker and John R. Kohlenberger (Grand Rapids, MI: Zondervan, 1994), 542–43.

[2] Robert Jamieson, A. R. Fausset, and David Brown, *A Commentary, Critical, Experimental, and Practical on the Old and New Testaments* (Grand Rapids, MI: Eerdmans, 1973), 381, note to 2 Kgs 4:42.

Elisha repeats his earlier command, he also now adds to it: "For thus said the LORD: They shall eat and have some left over" (4:43b). This is all that Elisha does: he orders the food to be given to the people and he conveys the word of the Lord.

Elisha does *not* multiply the loaves. Instead, Elisha trusts the word of the Lord and, in doing so, teaches the people to trust the Lord's word, too. As we might read in the psalms: "These all look to you, to give them their food in due season. When you give to them, they gather it up; when you open your hand, they are filled with good things" (Ps 104:27-28, RSV). Or again: "The LORD is faithful in all his words, and gracious in all his deeds. . . . The eyes of all look to you [Lord], and you give them their food in due season. You open your hand, you satisfy the desire of every living thing" (Ps 145:13b, 15-16, RSV). The meal Elisha provides to the people is trust in the word of God. It is God who feeds his people, taking the little loaves that are offered and creating from them an abundance of bread.

The Point

The bread is not the point. Yes, the hundred starving people surrounding Elisha need something to eat. Yes, the abundant bread fills their stomachs, and then some. And yes, the Lord responded to the immediate need of his people, a need for bread. But the real point is about who you can trust to care for all your needs.

Who can you turn to, in season and out of season? Who knows your needs even better than you do? What the Israelites once slowly learned in the desert as they gathered manna each morning, the people surrounding Elisha learn again here: "man does not live by bread alone, but . . . by everything that proceeds out of the mouth of the LORD" (Deut 8:3, RSV; cf. Matt 4:4). Bread comes and goes, but the word of the Lord is forever. Elisha's "miracle" is the trust in the word of the Lord in the midst of a hungry and often fickle people.

From this view, the small and seemingly less significant story at the end of this cycle of stories stands forth with greater prominence. The one who helped lift a widow out of poverty, who told a childless mother she would have a son and helped bring that same child back to life, and who purified poisoned food for his disciples is the one who trusts in the word of God.[3] That is the power of God's prophet, Elisha: he trusts in God's word, and he witnesses to the fidelity of God in the midst of the people.

---

[3] For more on this, see especially the sections on 2 Kgs 4 in Drew S. Holland, "1–2 Kings," in *Wesley One Volume Commentary*, ed. Kenneth J. Collins and Robert W. Wall (Nashville: Abingdon, 2020), 216–36.

The Abundant Bread 65

Guiding Your Child to Engage "The Abundant Bread"

Overview

A Look from Above

This final episode from the Old Testament is the fourth in a row that focuses on bread. From the Passover, the Israelites prepared unleavened bread for their journey (chapter 3); in the desert, the Lord gave his people manna: bread from heaven (chapter 4); and when he was exhausted and desperate in fear, Elijah received bread from the angel (chapter 5). After this session, we move to the first of the six episodes in the gospels, when connections to each of these six Old Testament episodes will deepen our understanding of and appreciation for Jesus' actions. In fact, the episode to which this one about Elisha's "abundant bread" will most especially connect is the very first one we encounter in the gospels: the feeding of the five thousand (chapter 7).

A Closer Look

Elisha is Elijah's successor. Part of the mission that Elijah received from the Lord at Mount Horeb was to anoint Elisha. Focusing now on Elisha is, in that sense, continuing to follow the mission of Elijah. This is a very brief passage but one where we have to pay extra attention to see what is and is not taking place. It is tempting to see this as Elisha multiplying bread because we are so familiar with the story of Jesus doing so. That is not what happens here. Instead, Elisha places his trust in the word of God and leads others to do the same.

1st Movement—Welcoming the Word of God

1. Opening Prayer

2. Quick Review

    Especially since this episode with Elisha follows (after some time) the story and mission of Elijah, it is good to review 1 Kings 19 and "the prophet's strength." As always, it is best to use your child's drawing of that episode to help with the review, if possible. The following four points are most important for this review:

- Elijah started off very afraid and very tired, as the whole army of Israel was after him.
- God sent his angel to Elijah to give him strength when he was afraid and tired, bringing him bread and water in the desert.
- With that strength from the bread of the angel, Elijah traveled very, very far to meet the Lord in the silence. Elijah knew God's presence in his heart.
- When the Lord met Elijah, he gave Elijah a new mission and new courage.

2*nd* Movement—Engaging the Word of God

1. Set the Scene

   Very briefly, introduce Elisha as a different prophet from Elijah. Elisha is the one who comes right after Elijah, to continue Elijah's work as a prophet. Part of the mission Elijah received from God was to anoint Elisha as the next prophet. This story takes place after Elisha has taken over for Elijah in Israel.

2. Reading

   2 Kgs 4:42-44. Read the passage through slowly, out loud.

3. Questions about the Reading

   After you finish reading the passage once, consider the following questions. Since the passage is so brief, it is possible to remember the details from one reading, but chances are you will need to read through each line again with your child to talk about what is asked below.

   - What is the problem that Elisha is facing in this story? (Pay attention to what his servant or attendant says in verse 43.)
     - Notice that there are one hundred men who need to be fed. The problem is that the people are hungry and there is not enough food.

- What has the man from Baal-shalishah brough to Elisha?
  - See from the text that this man has brought twenty loaves.
  - Help your child to understand that each of these loaves is very, very small—so small that each one would be like a little snack for one person. Clearly, there is not nearly enough for one hundred people!
  - Perhaps you might also point out that the bread the man brought is from the "first reaping" which means that it is the portion that is typically offered to God. The man has made a gift to God by giving this bread to Elisha.
- So what does Elisha do now that he has just a little bit of bread and a lot of hungry people?
  - Note that Elisha does two things. First, he *immediately* tells his servant to give the bread to the hungry people. Second, when the servant says that the food is not enough, Elisha tells him again to give it to the people and now says that the Lord has promised that there will be some left over!
  - It is important to stress that *Elisha does not multiply the bread*. Instead, Elisha gives the bread to the people and trusts the word of God.
- What happens, in the end?
  - Simply put: everyone eats and is filled, and there is some left over.
  - Crucial: what the Lord promised is done.

4. Points to Emphasize

With this very brief passage, it is really important to stress these crucial points:

- The problem is that the people are hungry but there is not enough bread.
- The prophet Elisha does *not* multiply the bread.
- The prophet Elisha trusts in the word of God, and leads others to do the same.

- The bread is important here, but what is more important is trusting in God. This is like the Israelites in the desert and the manna: the important thing there was that they trust the Lord to feed them, every day.
- (If your child notices a forthcoming connection to Jesus multiplying the loaves and fishes, that's great! If not, you may or may not choose to see if you can tease that out of your child with some leading questions, but don't worry about it if not.)

3rd Movement—Reflecting on the Word of God

1. Activity

   Draw the scene.

2. Discussion

   Ask your child to tell you about the drawing.

3. Closing Prayer

chapter seven

Jesus Feeds the Five Thousand

(Mark 6:30-44)

My children have lived their entire lives around the University of Notre Dame. They have spent more time on that college campus than most enrolled students. When I took our oldest child to visit other college campuses as a prospective student, he eventually came to see all those other campuses in relation to the one he knew best. He immediately saw the similarities in some regarding the residential nature of campus, or the layout of dining halls, or the size or feel of the place. Those similarities then became the basis for identifying the differences: though this new one shared this particular quality with the one he previously knew (Notre Dame), it actually was different because of this other thing. Rather than each experience of visiting other college campuses being an encounter with a totally new and foreign thing, each one had some sense of familiarity that then highlighted its own distinctive features more. It was the similarities that made the differences more apparent.

In the movement from the Old Testament episodes of the Lord feeding his people to the episodes in the gospels, something like that can and should take place. The more attentive and open we are, the more we should feel like we have seen something like this before. It should feel familiar. And yet, that familiarity is not evidence of redundancy, but rather fulfillment. What we find in the gospels is Jesus fulfilling, in and through himself, all of the ways in which God feeds his people. Jesus is God-with-us; in him, we encounter the giver and the gift as one. The similarities we can and should notice with the Old

The Sheep and the Shepherd

Jesus' apostles had just returned from their mission of preaching and healing, full of stories and totally exhausted. Wanting to give them rest apart from the great many people, Jesus took them away to "a lonely place" for a retreat (Mark 6:31, 32).[1] But the crowds saw them and followed, such that "a great throng" awaited them (Mark 6:34). This meant that the lonely place was filled with people.

Before he does anything to, with, or for this "great throng" that followed him and his apostles to this lonely place, Jesus first sees them. He sees them with compassion. He sees their condition. He sees that "they [are] like sheep without a shepherd" (Mark 6:34). That is far from coincidental terminology. This people appears to Jesus the way in which Israel had appeared after the demise of one of their kings, or while they were under the rule of a wicked or inept king.[2] Jesus sees their true spiritual condition. This act of seeing is the first thing we learn about Jesus in relation to the crowd.

In Israel's history, when the people fall into such a desperate condition, it is always the Lord who comes to their aid. He comes directly, and he comes through the work of his servants, the prophets. The Lord gives the people what they need, in terms of both their immediate needs and their everlasting needs. In the near term, sheep need food, water, and a pasture. In the long term, sheep need a shepherd who will care for them, always guiding them to what they need. If Jesus sees this people as "sheep without a shepherd," what does that mean about what they need? Soon, of course, we learn that they need to be fed, but their deeper and lasting need goes well beyond one meal.

They are sheep without a shepherd, so Jesus teaches them. He gives them his words, his wisdom, his teaching. This is Jesus' immediate

---

[1] All biblical quotations in this chapter come from the RSV translation, unless otherwise noted.

[2] Richard B. Hays, *Echoes of Scripture in the Gospels* (Waco, TX: Baylor University Press, 2016), 69. For examples of Israel presented in these terms, see 1 Kgs 22:17; 2 Chr 18:16; Zech 10:2; Jdt 11:19.

response to seeing them as they are. "He had compassion on them . . . and he began to teach them many things" (Mark 6:34). If he sees what they really need and he then teaches them, they must really need what comes forth from his mouth.

But who is this Jesus, who sees with compassion and teaches with authority? In ages past, it was the Lord who promised to lead the people out of their desperation and bring them into his care, providing them with protection and sustenance.[3] When Moses neared the end of his life, he prayed to the Lord to appoint a leader in his place so that the people would not be "like sheep without a shepherd" (see Num 27:15-17). Is Jesus another Moses—a successor to Moses, just like Moses—who leads the people at God's behest? Yes, and no.

The Lord's response to the people's condition is stronger and more direct than even Moses prayed for. Through the prophet Ezekiel, the LORD God himself declared that "I, I myself will search for my sheep, and will seek them out . . . I will rescue them from all places where they have been scattered . . . I will feed them with good pasture . . . I myself will be the shepherd of my sheep" (Ezek 34:11, 12, 14, 15). Jesus sees that the people are like "sheep without a shepherd"; what they really need is a shepherd; the Lord has pledged himself as the shepherd of this people. Moses asked for someone to take his place, and the Lord responds by pledging himself. Jesus himself is the answer to Moses' prayer and the Lord's pledge. Jesus is the divine shepherd.

A Miracle in a Lonely Place

As Jesus teaches the people, the apostles get concerned. The hour has grown late. The people are hungry and growing hungrier. There is nothing available for them in this "lonely place." The apostles arrive at a reasonable conclusion: they must send the people somewhere else to find the food they need.

Jesus responds to this reasonable conclusion with a seemingly unreasonable command: "You give them something to eat" (Mark 6:37). The apostles are flabbergasted. These are the same apostles who have just recently returned from their mission of preaching and healing in

---

[3] Hays, *Echoes of Scripture*, 69.

the name of Jesus, on his own authority, but now that he commands them to give the people something to eat, they look at him dumbfounded. This is a lonely place, there is nothing here, there is no way to feed them. What's more, were they to procure the food to feed such a number of people, the cost would be outrageous. A single denarius is a full day's wage. To buy enough to feed this many people would cost two hundred denarii, which is more than half a year's salary!

Jesus answers the apostles' incredulity with a question and a more limited command: "How many loaves have you? Go and see" (Mark 6:38). They return to him with five loaves and two fish. Five loaves and two fish is ridiculous in the midst of five thousand people who hunger. Yet Jesus persists, organizing the people into groups on the "green grass," as a shepherd would arrange his sheep in a pasture (see Mark 6:39), and then he begins preparing food for them by taking the loaves and fish in his hands. Indeed, as the gospel writer tells us, Jesus takes, blesses, and breaks the bread, then he gives the food to his disciples to give to the people. Take, bless, break, give: that is the fourfold action of Jesus at the Last Supper (Mark 14:22; see also Luke 24:30-31).

Jesus is the one who acts. He first teaches the people; then he commands his disciples and the people; then he takes, blesses, breaks, and gives the bread. And when all had eaten, there were leftovers. Jesus multiplied the bread and the fish by the work of his own hands. Whose hands are those? Who is this man, Jesus? He is known by what he does: he is the one who sees with compassion, who teaches, who feeds and cares for. The people are in need of a shepherd—by what he does, Jesus reveals himself as the shepherd they've been waiting for. Jesus is the Lord who shepherds his people: he knows them and they are coming to know him.[4]

The people receive the bread and the fish, and the apostles receive a renewal of their own identity and mission. When Jesus the shepherd feeds his sheep, he gives the food to his disciples to give to the people. Jesus enlists the disciples in his reign of care. They are ministers of his care, though it is indeed *his* care. He feeds the people, and he gives the apostles the dignity and the responsibility of serving his mission. This is what they had just returned from doing before they left for that

---

[4] Hays, *Echoes of Scripture*, 70.

lonely place, and here in the lonely place he forms them more deeply in their mission, in response to their own doubts and incredulity.

When everything is accomplished, there are leftovers. The leftovers are gathered up into twelve baskets. There is one basket for each of the twelve apostles. There is one apostle for each of the twelve tribes of Israel. The leftovers themselves are a sign of wholeness and completion: one people of Israel though twelve tribes, one identity and mission in Jesus though twelve apostles. Twelve baskets from this one meal, this one work, this one miracle in a lonely place.

Jesus Beyond Elisha

Elisha was surrounded by a lot of hungry people. There were one hundred of them. Theirs was a time of famine, when the place where they lived did not produce what was needed to sustain life. Yet, someone came forward from another place and offered the best portion of the little bit that he had: he gave twenty loaves of barley bread. Each loaf was only enough for a light snack. There were too many people and nowhere near enough food.

Elisha commanded that the bread be given to the people nonetheless. It seemed reckless and naive: what good would so little do against the need of so many? But Elisha insisted. Even more, he pledged his trust in the word of the Lord, for the Lord promises to feed his people. In fact, the Lord promises that when he feeds, there will be leftovers. What Elisha really gave was his trust in the word of God. His attendant and the people witnessed that trust.

After the people had eaten and were filled, there was leftover bread. There was too little bread to begin with, but at the end there is evidence of more than enough. Elisha did not multiply the bread: all he did was trust in the Lord and incline the others to do the same. Elisha was the servant, the prophet, the herald and the witness of the Lord's action.

Jesus *is* the Lord's action. He was surrounded by *more* hungry people than Elisha was, and he saw that what they really needed was a shepherd. Their immediate need for bread was not everything, though that need mattered to Jesus. Even with a great number of hungry people, Jesus had in his hands even less than Elisha had. Whereas Elisha took the little he had and gave it to the people with his trust that the Lord would provide, Jesus takes the very little offered and by the work of his own hands multiplies the offering so that it becomes far more than enough. In fact, the leftovers from Jesus' work are themselves a sign of wholeness—those twelve baskets. What was revealed in that lonely place is the importance of trusting Jesus: he is the one who feeds with his words and with his actions. He himself is the answer to Elisha's act of trust: Jesus is the Lord feeding his people, abundantly.

Guiding Your Child to Engage "Jesus Feeding the Five Thousand"

Overview

A Look from Above

Having completed one session on each of the six Old Testament episodes, this is the first session dedicated to an episode with Jesus in the gospels. Moving into the gospels does not mean leaving the Old Testament behind. On the contrary, we read the gospels better if we read them in harmony with the Old Testament. Starting with this particular gospel episode immediately after the session on Elisha and the abundant bread helps to make the connection even more apparent. Both episodes concern feeding many people from what is initially too little. One of the hopes of these next six sessions is that we help our children grow in seeing Scripture as one complete, unfolding mystery of God's care for his people.

A Closer Look

The feeding of the five thousand is likely a familiar episode. Familiarity can aid understanding, but it can also obstruct understanding if we assume we know too much from the start. Seeing this episode against the backdrop of Elisha's deed should help to highlight the differences, which leads to a deeper appreciation of Jesus' uniqueness. The condition of the people, the precise actions of Jesus, the depiction of the apostles, and even the specifics of the leftovers are all meaningful and thus emphasized here.

1ˢᵗ *Movement—Welcoming the Word of God*

1. Opening Prayer

2. Quick Review

    The similarities and differences with 2 Kings 4:42-44 are important for this session, so a quick review of Elisha and the abundant bread is in order. As always, it is best to use your child's drawing of that episode to help with the review, if possible. The following three points are most important:

- The prophet Elisha was surrounded by many hungry people and he did not have anywhere near enough bread (one hundred people, twenty small loaves of bread).
- Elisha did not multiply the bread; instead, he gave what he had to the people with his trust that the Lord would provide.
- When everyone had eaten, there were leftovers.

2nd Movement—Engaging the Word of God

1. Set the Scene

   It would be wise to say something about beginning to read the gospels, where Jesus is always the main figure. All the episodes that came before were during the time of waiting for Jesus. Starting today, all the episodes are from the time when Jesus has finally come.

2. Reading

   Mark 6:30-44. Read the passage through slowly, out loud.

3. Questions about the Reading

   After you finish reading the passage once, we can begin with one general question and then several more focused questions, each of which relate to a different part of the narrative.

   - What does this story remind you of?
     - As much as possible, allow your child to make connections with the story about Elisha.
     - You may also ask your child what is different about this story compared with Elisha's.
   - Jesus takes his apostles away, but lots of people follow them. When Jesus sees all those people, what do they look like to him? (See 6:34.)

- Note that Jesus thinks the people are like "sheep without a shepherd."
- Talk about what happens to sheep without a shepherd: they get lost and confused, and they can't feed themselves.
- If they are sheep without a shepherd, what do they need most of all? A shepherd.
- (Note: "apostles" and "disciples" seem to be interchangeable terms in this narrative.)

- When it gets late, what are the disciples worried about? And what does Jesus tell them? (See 6:36-37.)
  - Notice that the disciples are worried that the people are hungry and that there is no food.
  - Notice that Jesus tells them to give the people something to eat.
  - Notice that the disciples think what Jesus says is crazy because it would take so much food to feed this many people and there is hardly anything in this place.
  - Point: The disciples do not fully trust Jesus.

- What does Jesus do to feed all these people? (See 6:38-41.)
  - Note: it is important to move step by step here. Perhaps go line by line and talk about each thing that Jesus does.
  - First, Jesus tells his disciples to bring him all the food that is around. They find five loaves and two fish.
  - Second, Jesus organizes the people into groups on the grass. He is acting like a shepherd who puts his sheep in order in a pasture (green grass!).
  - Third, Jesus *takes* the loaves and fish, *blesses* them, *breaks* them, and *gives* them to the disciples to give to the people. This fourfold action is crucial: take, bless, break, give.
  - Note: the disciples who doubted are now the ones whom Jesus makes into servants to feed the people.

- How many people were there? Was there enough food in the end? (See 6:42-44.)
    - Note: there were five thousand people (6:44). That is *way* more than Elisha had to feed.
    - Note: everyone ate until they were full *and* there was food left over.
    - Note: there are twelve baskets left over, one for each of the twelve apostles.

4. Points to Emphasize

   These are some of the main points to emphasize, either as you go along or at the end:

   - The people are like sheep without a shepherd, so Jesus becomes a shepherd for them: teaching them, feeding them, caring for them. Jesus is the Good Shepherd.
   - Like Elisha, Jesus is surrounded by many hungry people. Unlike Elisha, Jesus is the one who multiplies the bread and fish. Jesus does what Elisha trusted God to do.
   - The fourfold action of Jesus with the bread—take, bless, break, give—is exactly what he will do at the Last Supper. *This is the most important point.*
   - The leftovers are in twelve baskets. There are twelve apostles because there are twelve tribes of Israel. This tells us that Jesus is caring for the whole people of God.

3rd Movement—Reflecting on the Word of God

1. Activity

   Draw the scene.

2. Discussion

   Ask your child to tell you about the drawing.

3. Closing Prayer

chapter eight

Jesus Turns Water to Wine at Cana

(John 2:1-11)

"They have no wine," and "Do whatever he tells you." That is all that the mother of Jesus says in the Gospel of John. In saying so little, she says everything.

This story is familiar. Jesus is at a wedding at Cana in Galilee along with his mother and disciples. They run out of wine. This is bad news for the guests, but even worse for the bride and groom who would be humiliated at not providing adequately for their guests. Mary tells Jesus, Jesus turns water into wine, the wine is really good, and the party goes on. Jesus is the savior . . . of parties.

Being known throughout the ages as the savior of parties is a pretty exalted title, but of course John the Evangelist does not recount this event for us merely to confer that honor upon Jesus. By the end of the episode we are told that what happened at that wedding feast was "the first of his signs [which] manifested his glory; and his disciples believed in him" (John 2:11).[1] What takes place at Cana is a sign of something greater. His disciples recognized the sign and their response was belief. What exactly did his disciples *see*? Yes, they saw wine where there had been no wine, but they also saw the effectiveness of Mary's words. The wine and the words are about more than the party.

---

[1] All biblical quotations in this chapter come from the RSV translation, unless otherwise noted.

Between Mary and Jesus

As with most of the episodes in the gospels—and especially those in the Gospel of John—Jesus is definitely at the center of this episode at Cana. But he only takes center stage here in verse 6. In the first three verses, the focus is placed more squarely on his mother, even to the point that John begins by saying that she was there at the wedding before stating that "Jesus also was invited" (2:2), like he was her "plus one." Moreover, the unnamed Mary is the first to speak: "They have no wine" (2:3). When Jesus speaks, it is in response to her: "O woman, what have you to do with me? My hour has not yet come" (2:4). When Mary speaks again and for the last time, it is as if her words not only instruct those to whom she directly speaks but even redirect the focus of the narrative itself: "Do whatever he tells you" (2:5). She moves the focus onto her son. Whatever he does and whatever he says is the main focus.

The brief exchange between Mary and Jesus deserves thoughtful attention. The very first action of Mary in this gospel reveals two things at once: she sees what the particular need is and she brings that need to Jesus. The initial description of her is of one who observes what is lacking and seeks to do something about it. Jesus' response, though, strikes us as peculiar, even off-putting. It sounds like Jesus denies or at least pushes back against his mother's concern. He tells her that it is not his time, his "hour." By the end of this gospel, we learn that his hour is when he reveals his glory in full—the glory of his Father (see John 17:1-19). That hour will have to do with his passion, death, and resurrection, by which he is fully revealed for who he is. To perform a miracle, he would begin to reveal his glory before the appointed time. Mary's response to this seeming rebuff? "Do whatever he tells you."

Clearly, Jesus does something about the lack of wine; he directs the servants. In some way that neither they nor we see or know, once they do what he tells them they discover that the six stone jars that were filled with water are now filled with wine. When the steward tastes that wine, he discovers that it is in fact the best wine.[2] The servants

---

[2] The steward's ignorance over the origin of the wine is possibly an echo of the ignorance of many to where Jesus himself is from, which is a major theme in John's gospel, as we have already seen in John 6 (D. Moody Smith, "John," in *The Harper-*

see what they see but do not understand. The steward tastes what he tastes but does not get it. The bridegroom is no doubt as confused as anyone at his own good fortune. What happened, and why?

All anyone can see is that Jesus told the servants to fill the jars with water and then draw some of that water out. When they did what he told them to do, there was wine. There is nothing else to see there: there is no further explanation as to what has taken place or how this change has occurred.

We must remember that the disciples saw something. They saw what took place as a sign, and by seeing it they "believed in him" (2:11). They saw that, somehow, by following Jesus' command, the servants found wine where there was previously only water, and the steward tasted the best wine when he would have expected the worst, and the bridegroom was put in line for praise when only a moment ago he was bound for humiliation. The disciples were witnesses to these things. But what they also saw was what started the whole thing: Jesus' mother brought the need to Jesus and directed the servants to do what he said to do.

Jesus' "hour" is when his glory will be revealed. Did the disciples not in fact witness the beginning of the revelation of God's glory here? The Son who is unfailingly obedient to his Father's will allows himself to be moved by the plea of his mother. He lets *her* concern affect him, even to the point of seeming to act before his time. If they saw that, then the disciples witnessed something about the otherwise unthinkable power of God: this is a God who is not trapped in his own grandeur, but who is willing to bend down to *listen to his creatures*, like a son listens to his mother. The work that is performed is indeed a divine work—the water is not changed into wine by human power. But by exercising his divine power in response to his mother's plea, Jesus makes her intercession meaningful and effective.[3]

Collins Bible Commentary, ed. James L. Mays [San Francisco: HarperSanFrancisco, 2000], 961). Furthermore, the wine may be read as a sign of Jesus himself, who is "the best wine" that has come at the end of salvation history (D. Moody Smith, *John*, Abingdon New Testament Commentaries [Nashville: Abingdon, 1999], 85).

[3] For more on the mystery of Mary's plea and Jesus' action, see Leonard J. DeLorenzo, *A God Who Questions* (Huntington, IN: Our Sunday Visitor, 2019),

The sign Jesus performs is a revelation of his Father in heaven and his mother on earth. In Jesus, God hears and acts on the needs of his people, just as in Jesus, the faith and works of God's people help usher in the glory of God.[4] Mary made a real offering. She was not the only one who knew the wine had run out, but she was the only one who turned immediately and with confidence to Jesus with her need. She did not ask for a particular work; she merely brought the need to him. She trusted him. By confessing the need to Jesus and directing others in confidence to him, she said and did all that needed to be said and done.

Between the Sign and What Is to Come

The servants brought forth water and received wine in exchange. At the Last Supper, Jesus will take the cup that has been provided and give it back to his disciples as the blood of his new covenant. At every Mass, God's people bring forth the fruit of the vine and the work of human hands, and receive back the blood of Jesus: the love of God poured out for the world.

The simple but direct offering of Mary to present both the needs of others and her own trust to Jesus finds a response in the divine work Jesus performs. She reveals her faith in him and he reveals the glory of God. There is a mutual sacrifice between them, by which God makes space in his great deeds for our humble offerings. God makes our prayers matter in and through Jesus.

To see the whole sign at Cana requires us to see both the change of water to wine *and* the way in which God allows prayer to be folded into the good done in Jesus. If the disciples saw what took place at Cana as a *sign* that led them to believe, they saw this grand mystery taking place. It is more than a matter of seeing the bare details of the event; it is also about seeing with the eyes of faith. They saw that this man, Jesus, is the Word of God united to human flesh. He is the one in whom the Creator becomes one with his creatures, taking on their

---

67–73; and Leonard DeLorenzo, *Into the Heart of the Father: Learning from and Giving Yourself through Christ in Prayer* (Frederick, MD: Word Among Us, 2021), 101–3.

[4] DeLorenzo, *Into the Heart of the Father*, 103.

needs and condition as his own. And it all begins with his union with his mother.

Between the Forbidden Fruit and the Choicest Wine

Did you notice that Jesus calls his mother "Woman"? To our modern ears, this may sound at least strange if not disrespectful. In the ancient world, though, it is often an address of affection and respect. Even still, we would be hard pressed to find precedent in antiquity for a son calling his mother "woman." This is not at all common in ancient literature, let alone the Bible.

And yet there is precedent in the Bible for this address—not between son and mother, but between the original companions in Genesis. When the *'adam* sees the companion whom the LORD God has created from his side, he rejoices and calls her "Woman" (Gen 2:23). That name is a name of relation, as the man also renames himself in relation to her just as he proclaims her name in relation to himself (*'ish* and *'ishshah*, or "Man" and "Woman"). By the LORD God's providential plan, they were created for one another, to be companions to one another, to live together in fidelity and intimacy, to lead one another and grow together toward all that is good.

What happened, of course, is that rather than leading each other into truth, they led each other into disobedience as they clothed themselves in deception. The woman reached out and took the forbidden fruit and gave it to her husband, who consumed it without deliberation. But here, at the wedding at Cana, something else is taking place. Jesus receives the concern of his mother and, in the fullness of deliberation, follows her word and thereby brings her along in his mission of obedience to his Father's will. The choicest wine given by God for the guests at Cana is, at the same time, the consecrated fruit of the harmonious union between this woman and this man, who is her son and the Son of the Father. He calls her "Woman" because the original goodness of humanity is being restored.

Guiding Your Child to Engage "Jesus Turning the Water to Wine"

Overview

A Look from Above

This is the second of our three gospel episodes set during Jesus' years of ministry, alongside the feeding of the five thousand (chapter 7) and the bread of life discourse (chapter 9). Though not as obvious or explicit as the connection between Elisha's abundant bread and Jesus feeding the five thousand, the Old Testament connection for the wedding at Cana is the forbidden fruit in the Garden of Eden (chapter 2). Here, the harmony between Mary and Jesus is the redemption of the disobedience of Eve and Adam.

A Closer Look

Mary plays a crucial role in this episode as the one who brings the problem to Jesus and the one who directs everyone to follow his word. The theme of abundance continues with the quantity of wine, though now the *quality* of the gift is also emphasized. We will recognize the water that Jesus turns to wine as a symbol of the wine through which he gives his blood at the Last Supper, in the Eucharist.

1st Movement—Welcoming the Word of God

1. Opening Prayer

2. Quick Review

    The time spent on Genesis 3 with the forbidden fruit is, by this time, many weeks behind us. It is important to refresh the memory of that episode here, preferably (as always) by using your child's drawing to show the way. There are at least three main points that should in some way be part of this review.

    - The first man and woman follow the serpent in distrusting God and God's word.
    - They *take* the forbidden fruit and are *ashamed*.

Jesus Turns Water to Wine at Cana 85

- They do *not* receive from the Lord but try to do what they want by themselves.

2nd *Movement—Engaging the Word of God*

1. Reading

   John 2:1-11. Read the passage through slowly, out loud.

2. Questions about the Reading

   After you finish reading the passage once, a short series of questions and small teaching points will help to deepen the understanding of the episode.

   - Question: Jesus, Mary, and the disciples are at a wedding. What is the problem?
     - Answer: They have run out of wine.
     - Note: You might teach how running out of wine would have been a huge embarrassment to the bride and groom who are hosting the party.
   - Question: Who notices the problem and tells Jesus about it?
     - Answer: His mother.
     - Point: Mary sees what's wrong and she goes to Jesus with the problem. She trusts Jesus and tells everyone else to do whatever he says.
   - Question: What does Jesus do after his mother tells everyone to listen to him?
     - Answer: He does two things. First, he tells the servants to fill the stone jars with water (emphasize how large these jars are). Second, he tells the servants to draw some water out of the jars and bring it to the head waiter. That's it.
   - Question: It says that the water in the jars had become wine, but how did that happen?
     - Answer: We are not told *how* it happened, only that Jesus told them what to do and when they did it, the water turned into the wine they needed.
     - Point: Listening to Jesus is what matters here.

- Question: What did the head waiter say when he tasted the wine?
  - Answer: He said it was the best wine, better than what they usually had.
  - Point: When they didn't have any wine, Jesus gave them so much (six stone jars full) of the best wine.

3. Points to Emphasize

   These are some of the main points to emphasize in summary, at the end:

   - Mary trusts in Jesus and asks Jesus for what the people need. Think about how Mary offers *our* needs to Jesus, like we ask in the Hail Mary (". . . pray for us sinners, now and at the hour of our death").
   - In the Garden of Eden the man and woman did not listen to God's word but *took* what they wanted instead. At the wedding in Cana, Mary led everyone to listen to Jesus' word and they *received* what is best from him.
   - Key 1: Here Jesus turns water to wine; later at the Last Supper he will turn wine into his own blood.
   - Key 2: Just like the servants at the wedding bring Jesus water and he gives it back to them as wine, at Mass we bring wine to the altar and Jesus gives it back to us as his own blood.

3rd Movement—Reflecting on the Word of God

1. Activity

   Draw the scene.

2. Discussion

   Ask your child to tell you about the drawing.

3. Closing Prayer

chapter nine

Jesus Is the Bread of Life

(John 6:25-38, 41-42, 48-58)

The people who ate after Jesus multiplied the loaves and fish must have really liked their meal. They ended up following him to the other side of the lake the next day and, according to Jesus, they sought him out because he had given them food (see John 6:22-26). I can relate. When I was in my first year of college, I meandered to the tailgating lots before the first home football game. The experience for a first-year student was dull. But then, at some point in the middle of the season, my friends and I happened upon a tailgate with some very generous older alumni. They insisted we come eat with them. The chicken fingers and cookies were seemingly endless. We stuffed ourselves, and still they had more food. You better believe that the very next football Saturday we headed directly to that same parking spot, hoping to be fed again. Had there been a lake between our dorm and that parking spot, we would have sprinted around or even swam across it. We would have done anything for free food.

Like my friends and me, the people who benefited from the food Jesus multiplied made the trek because they wanted more benefits. Like us, they did not seek their donor out of gratitude or a sense of friendship. Like us, they wanted more of the food they had received. It is important to remember, however, that when Jesus saw these people as "sheep without a shepherd" (according to Mark's gospel), he first taught them. The food came later. What they needed was both the teaching and the victuals, and Jesus gave them both. The main thing, though, was that they needed a shepherd: Jesus himself. But they set their appetites on the bread rather than on him who gave them bread.[1] Their desires were out of whack, as Jesus tells them: "Truly, truly, I say to you, you seek me, not because you saw signs, but because you ate your fill of the loaves. Do not labor for the food which perishes, but for the food which endures to eternal life, which the Son of man will give to you" (John 6:26-27).[2]

In the discussion that follows the main question is what exactly Jesus gives and what the people desire, or are willing to learn to desire. It is indeed a matter of bread, but not as the people imagine.

What the People Want

When the people received the bread on the other side of the lake, their vision was set on the bread, not on the sign that the bread was. This is what Jesus tells them at the beginning of this encounter. To see the bread but fail to see the sign means they failed to see how that bread both revealed something about the giver and pointed to something greater than what they already received.

Were the people so focused on the meal they received to fill their empty stomachs that they neglected to notice the fact that the man who provided it to them created that abundance out of an astonishingly small offering? There were five loaves and two fish, and yet he made enough to feed five thousand people! To receive a share in that bounteous meal ought to have caused each person to look up and wonder at who this man is—this man that fed them by such a deed. And if they were to wonder at this man who fed them so miraculously, meeting their immediate need with overwhelming generosity, might they not have also wondered at what greater gift this man might be for them, or what greater need he might meet beyond this present need of empty stomachs? In other words, ought not that bread have been pondered as a sign of both the power of the one who gave it and the possibility of greater gifts to come?

After Jesus calls them out for the error of their sight and desire, he speaks of food that will not pass away but endures. The people are

---

[1] See D. Moody Smith, *John*, Abingdon New Testament Commentaries (Nashville: Abingdon, 1999), 151–52.

[2] All biblical quotations in this chapter come from the RSV translation, unless otherwise noted.

intrigued. They want to know how they can labor for *that* food. Jesus tells them to believe in the one whom God has sent. They recognize that Jesus is talking about himself and they seem prepared to believe that Jesus is the one from God, but only if he meets *their* expectations.[3] They thus ask him what sign he might perform so that they might believe in him. He must prove it to them. That is a very funny thing to demand, since it further ignores his previous "sign" of feeding the five thousand. They persist, therefore, in missing that earlier sign, not to mention that they fail to truly ponder the curious fact that Jesus had made his way across the lake without a boat (see 6:22).

When they ask for a sign from this man, Jesus, they throw down the gauntlet. They say that when their ancestors were hungry in the desert and complained to Moses, they received manna in response: "He gave them bread from heaven to eat" (6:31). They want to know what Jesus can give them, since Moses gave their ancestors manna. Can Jesus stack up to Moses' deed? As is his custom, Jesus responds in such a way that he calls the very premise of their query into question.

Jesus corrects or at least clarifies what they themselves have said: "it was not Moses who gave you bread from heaven" (6:32a). Surely, though, the people would agree, when prodded, that it was God indeed who ultimately gave the bread. But what they are not at all prepared to hear and what is truly shocking is that Jesus does not merely say "God" gave the bread, but rather "my Father" (6:32b). This changes the terms.

Jesus is claiming the one who gave the manna as *his* Father. Even more, Jesus has changed the tense of the verb. It is no longer what *was* given, but now what "my Father *gives* you." And so, by his response to the people, Jesus has introduced a double revelation: first, *his* Father is the giver of what comes down from heaven, and second, the manna previously given was a sign of what is now coming. What is now coming is a different kind of bread altogether. In sum, Jesus reinterprets the manna as having prefigured or anticipated *himself*.[4]

---

[3] D. Moody Smith, "John," in *The HarperCollins Bible Commentary*, ed. James L. Mays (San Francisco: HarperSanFrancisco, 2000), 968.

[4] Richard B. Hays, *Echoes of Scripture in the Gospels* (Waco, TX: Baylor University Press, 2016), 322; see also Smith, *John*, 153, 159.

Jesus has now reset the terms. He is bringing the focus to what God is giving *now*, as he presses the question of what the people are willing to receive and set their hearts on. Once Jesus tells them that "the bread of God . . . gives life to the world" (6:33), they respond with the plea that he "give us this bread always" (6:34). But will they accept the bread that is given?

A Matter of Belief

Jesus does most of the talking in the rest of this episode, with a few important interjections from the people. What Jesus says may be divided into two parts. The first part runs from verse 35 through verse 47 and has mostly to do with the issue of belief. The second part begins with verse 48 and concludes with verse 58, having mostly to do with eating and drinking.[5]

The part of Jesus' address concerning belief opens with the words "I am the bread of life" (6:35) and ends with him saying, "he who believes has eternal life" (6:47). The whole speech is therefore about the matter of believing that Jesus *is* the bread of life. This is no simple matter.

The bread of life is the bread that God gives—the bread *his* Father gives—and which therefore comes down from heaven. By saying he is the bread of life, he is saying that he himself has come down from heaven. He does not just stipulate that, he declares it outright: "For I have come down from heaven" (6:38a). What started as a discussion about bread has quickly become a matter of where Jesus comes from, of who exactly he is.

Only moments ago those who were listening to him begged him to "give us this bread always" (6:34). Now that he has identified himself with this bread and, furthermore, declared that he himself has come down from heaven, the people "murmured" (6:41). Murmuring is always a bad thing in Scripture: it is an expression of distrust, lack of patience, and even disdain. Not coincidentally, it is also what the Israelites did in the desert one month after being freed from slavery, when they were hungry—they murmured against Moses and Aaron,

---

[5] This division is observed in the note for John 6:35-59 in *The Ignatius Catholic Study Bible: The New Testament* (San Francisco: Ignatius, 2010), 174.

and thus against the Lord himself. What their ancestors once did, the people in front of Jesus now do. They murmur because they seek bread, and yet they do not accept what Jesus himself has said. He claims to be from heaven, but they *know* where he is from. He is "the son of Joseph, whose father and mother we know" (6:42). He is, in other words, just like the rest of us—of human origin. They hold fast to what they (think they) know and refuse to accept Jesus on terms that conflict with their presumed knowledge.

The primary question here is, therefore, Who really *knows* Jesus? The people claim to know, or at least they claim to know what he *cannot* be. Jesus, however, declares that only those whom the Father draws to him know Jesus in truth. The Father is the one who really knows Jesus—*his* Father, in heaven. To know Jesus is to receive the gift of knowing him from his Father. This knowing is far more than a matter of seeing or even having access to the prior events of his life. Knowing him comes from the gift of believing that he is who he shows himself to be: the Son of the Father.

To fail or refuse to know Jesus as he is means failing or refusing to grasp "the true bread from heaven" (6:32). Only that belief opens the way to "eternal life" (6:47).

A Matter of Eating and Drinking

Right in the middle of his address, Jesus moves the discussion onto new terms, not leaving behind the matter of belief but building on it. Jesus signals this move to new terms by repeating the declaration with which he began: "I am the bread of life" (6:48). What follows is a series of invitations to eat Jesus' flesh and drink his blood.[6] The people are shocked; many are downright scandalized.

Jesus opens this part of his discourse by returning to what the people themselves had invoked: the gift of manna in the desert (6:31). That bread was a gift, but those who ate of it eventually died. The gift of bread that Jesus is offering—"living bread," bread that is alive and bread that is for living—will give everlasting life. Those who eat of this bread will not die as their ancestors who ate manna did. This sounds like a great opportunity for all those who are listening, until Jesus states very

---

[6] See again *Ignatius Catholic Study Bible*, 174.

plainly and quite directly: "the bread which I shall give for the life of the world is my flesh" (6:51).

There is no way around this statement: it is clearly not metaphorical and yet it is absolutely puzzling to his listeners: "How can this man give us his flesh to eat?" (6:52). Their astonishment and shock would only deepen when Jesus immediately adds to his declaration that those who are to have life within them must also "drink his blood" (6:53). If his flesh is ordinary human flesh—as they presume it is (see again 6:42)—then eating his flesh would be prohibited under the Judaic law. And if his blood were merely ordinary human blood, drinking it would be doubly prohibited, as even drinking the blood of animals was prohibited. Because at least many of his interlocutors have determined from the start that he is a man like any other man, these words sound totally ludicrous, even scandalous. All of this further presses the importance of those crucial questions: Who is he, really? What are his body and blood, really? What would it mean to receive him as he is in this act of consumption: eating and drinking *him*?

"As the living Father sent me, and I live because of the Father, so he who eats me will live because of me" (6:57). This one line cuts to the heart of the matter. The Father is the living God, by whom all things come to life and from whom all gifts flow. Jesus is the one who comes from the Father, who is the Son of the Father, who alone knows God as "*my* Father," and who lives as the Father lives: one in perfect unity. The life that is offered is nothing other and nothing less than the life of God: the life of the Father, in and through the Son. Those who receive the Son—who take him into themselves, who are nourished by his flesh and blood—receive the very life of God: the gift of the Father to the world in his Son (see John 3:16-17). Those who eat of Jesus live not on their own, but by the life of Jesus, who shares completely in the life of God the Father (see also John 17).[7]

To grasp this intellectually all at once is too much for those who are listening to Jesus. But the point here is not to "get the idea." The point, as Jesus says plainly, is to eat and drink. Receive him as true food, as true drink, and you will receive the life he gives. Trust him, and you will come to believe from receiving. This demands that those who are

---

[7] See Timothy P. O'Malley, *Real Presence: What Does It Mean and Why Does It Matter?* (Notre Dame, IN: Ave Maria, 2021), especially 28–29.

listening to him let go of what they think they know and what they think is possible, and start again from first trusting in him. Understanding grows from trust.

How people are to eat his flesh and drink his blood has not yet been disclosed. For those of us who know the whole gospel, we already sense the way in which what Jesus says here is completed in the Last Supper. He will give his body and blood completely upon that table and upon the cross, so that those who receive him in the bread and the wine receive the gift of who and what he is, who and what the Father gives.

And so we come, in the end, to answer the crucial questions on which this second part of his discourse turn:

- Who is Jesus, really? He is the one come down from heaven, from the Father (see 6:38; cf. 6:42).
- What are his body and his blood? The bread and drink given from heaven as the Father's gift, which confers not temporary but eternal life (6:50 and 6:56; cf. 6:52).
- What does receiving him as he is mean? It means having eternal life through belief (6:40), not just as an idea or concept, but rather bodily (6:58). It means receiving him with your whole self, for he gives all that he is. What he gives is the life of God.

Manna and the True Bread

This encounter is built, in large part, on the memory of manna given in the desert. Jesus says that through him the Father gives "true bread" rather than manna. This does not mean that manna was "false bread." Manna was instead a sign of that which was to come. It nourished the Israelites for forty years as they wandered in the desert, but those who ate that bread still eventually died. Not only did those who ate that bread eventually perish, but the manna itself was perishable: it melted away every morning if it was not collected and it turned foul if it was stored overnight (see Exod 16:19-20). One of the essential properties of manna was that it was ephemeral: it came but it went, it nourished but it rotted, it was for today but not for tomorrow.

"The bread of life" is that which gives life without limit. It is not only bread for today, though it is bread for today. It is bread given here and now, but not bread that will pass away if not collected. It is bread that does not rot. It is bread that is not some*thing* but rather some*one*, and that someone is the eternal Son of the Father.

Manna means "What is it?" (Exod 16:15). That question does not go away with the "bread of life." The difference now is that the question becomes not *what* but "*Who* is it?" More to the point, the question is, "Who is *Jesus*?" In the completion of this episode, Jesus addresses his disciples and eventually turns to Simon Peter to ask him if he will leave because of what Jesus has said. Simon Peter responds: "Lord, to whom shall we go? You have the words of eternal life; and we have believed, and have come to know, that you are the Holy One of God" (6:68-69). By remaining with him, they are coming to *believe* and to *know* who he is. They have trusted him, and by their trust Jesus is bringing them to understanding. That journey to knowing him as he is, for who he is, will only be complete in the passion, death, and resurrection, by which he will give himself to them—body and blood, soul and divinity—in the Eucharist.

Guiding Your Child to Engage "Jesus, the Bread of Life"

Overview

A Look from Above

This is the third and final gospel episode of our journey that is set during Jesus' years of ministry. At the Last Supper (chapter 10), Jesus delivers the gift that he says he is: the bread of life, the blood of salvation. Of all twelve sessions, this one may be the most difficult not only because the passage is so wordy, but also because what Jesus says is both so important and so difficult to receive: he means it when he says we must eat his flesh and drink his blood, but *how* we do that is not yet apparent. We are coming upon the mystery of the Eucharist. Moreover, the connection to the manna in the desert (chapter 4) is crucial here.

A Closer Look

In this bread of life discourse, Jesus draws attention more and more to his own body and blood. His listeners resist at every turn. Never is it more important to follow Jesus' lead than here, where he alone can teach what must be taught. He is the bread sent down from his Father in heaven; he is the true manna; he himself is the way to eternal life. Listening to him is completed in receiving his body and blood, and receiving his body and blood is the way to truly listen to and follow him.

1st Movement—Welcoming the Word of God

1. Opening Prayer

2. Quick Review

    There are really three episodes that are helpful to review here, but of those three the most important is the manna in the desert (Exod 16:1-35). As always, try to use your child's drawing to help with the review. For the manna, the key points include the following:

    - God gives his people bread from heaven, called manna.
    - The meaning of manna is "What is it?"

96 *Fed by the Lord*

- This bread is given to them daily; it is their daily bread.
- The point is to trust the Lord to feed you.

A quick review of the last two sessions might also be helpful:

- Jesus feeds the five thousand (Mark 6:30-44): Jesus feeds the people by taking, blessing, breaking, and giving the bread he multiplies.
- Jesus turns the water into wine at Cana (John 2:1-11): When the people have no wine, Jesus takes what they have (water) and gives them what they need (wine).

2nd Movement—Engaging the Word of God

1. Set the Scene

   Remember the feeding of the five thousand. This episode takes place right afterward (see John 6:22-24). The people follow Jesus because he gave them food and they are looking for more. Jesus now wants to give them the food that doesn't just fill their stomachs but gives them true life with God.

2. Discussing and Teaching while Reading

   Since this passage is so long, wordy, and (especially for a child) hard to follow, it is best to read it together in parts, with discussion and teaching mixed in. The following reading and discussion itinerary should serve you well.

   - Part 1: What the People Want (John 6:25-35)
     - Read John 6:25-27. Ask: What do the people want? But what does Jesus want to give them?
       - Answer: The people want more food like he gave them before, but Jesus wants to give them food that makes them one with God.
     - Read John 6:28-34. Follow this by guiding your child to see the following:
       - The people want Jesus to show them a sign—perform a miracle—so they can believe in him. But remember, he

just fed five thousand people with a little bread and a couple of fish!
- The people say that Moses fed the Israelites in the desert with manna. They want Jesus to do something like that.
- Jesus tells them that Moses didn't feed the people; God did. Jesus says that the bread God now gives brings life to the whole world.
- The people say they want *that* bread!
  ○ Read John 6:35. Ask: What does Jesus say this bread is?
- Answer: He says that *he* is the bread of life!
- Part 2: A Matter of Belief (John 6:41-42)
  ○ Read John 6:41-42. Ask: How do the people respond when Jesus says that he is the bread of life?
    - Answer: They do not believe him. He says he comes from heaven, but they say they know his father and mother.
    - Note: The real question here is whether or not Jesus comes from heaven. If he is just like everyone else, then what he is saying does not make sense. Only if he is "God from God" (the Son of God) does this all matter. In the next part we are going to see if Jesus really means what he says or not.
- Part 3: A Matter of Eating and Drinking (John 6:48-58)
  ○ Read John 6:48-51. Follow this by guiding your child to see the following:
    - Again, he says "I am the bread of life" (v. 48). He must really mean it!
    - He says that even though the Israelites of old ate manna in the desert, they still died. He says that those who eat the "bread of life" will not die but live forever (with God).
    - Jesus says that he is the true bread. Like manna, he himself is given to them by God in heaven. And like manna, he is their daily bread. But unlike manna, he gives eternal life: life that never ends.

- Remember that with the manna the thing that mattered most was that the people trust God to feed them, each day. Now with Jesus, the thing that matters most is that the people trust *him* to give them what they need.
    - Read John 6:52-58. Follow this by guiding your child to see the following:
        - The people do not understand Jesus; they do not believe him. They cannot see how he could possibly be food for them, or how he came down from heaven.
        - Jesus does not change what he said; he makes it stronger. He says that you must eat his body and drink his blood to have the life of God in you.
        - Jesus does *not* tell them *how* they will eat his body and drink his blood. We have to wait till later to see that at the Last Supper.
        - Jesus says that whoever receives his body and blood, receives the life of God. That is the best thing that God can offer: his own life.

3. Points to Emphasize

   Again, this is probably the most difficult episode of our whole journey. Boiling this down to a few key points is helpful.

   - Jesus says that he is the "bread of life" who comes down from heaven.
   - The people want regular bread, then they want manna, but Jesus says that he is like manna except that he gives eternal life whereas manna does not.
   - What really matters is eating his body and drinking his blood. Jesus does not yet show them how they eat his body and drink his blood.

3rd Movement—Reflecting on the Word of God

1. Activity

   Draw the scene.

2. Discussion

   Ask your child to tell you about the drawing.

3. Closing Prayer

chapter ten

Jesus Institutes the Eucharist at the Last Supper

(Luke 22:1-2, 14-20)

I grew up in a single parent household; my dad raised my brother and me. When I was a teenager and being characteristically obnoxious and unpleasant around the house, one of my dad's friends pulled me aside and said: "Someday you'll realize all that your dad has done for you." Several decades later, I am still coming to realize it more and more.

In addition to knowing my dad and me pretty well, this friend implicitly knew something else: you cannot always comprehend what is happening while it is happening. There are some events and experiences that require distance, reflection, time, and more maturity in order to recognize them for what they truly were and are. Being in the middle of something does not mean you understand what you are in the middle of at the time you are in the middle of it. And there are some events and experiences that you never get to the end of understanding since the meaning grows more and more as you learn to see more and more.

I think about things like that when I read this seemingly simple line near the beginning of the Last Supper narrative in the Gospel of Luke:

> And when the hour came, he sat at table, and the apostles [were] with him. (Luke 22:14)[1]

---

[1] All biblical quotations in this chapter come from the RSV translation, unless otherwise noted.

Those twelve apostles were there, in the middle of what took place in the upper room. They shared the last meal with Jesus before he died. No one else saw what they saw, heard what they heard, or felt what they felt. They are the ones who told others. And yet, how much did they grasp in the middle of it all, as it was happening? Maybe some of it, but not all. They themselves grew to understand this one meal more and more after the fact. There was too much going on in the moment to comprehend it all. In fact, too much happened there for them to ever get to the end of understanding what had taken place. There was always more to be grateful for; always deeper and richer ways to give thanks to the one who gave them bread and wine that night.

The Time and Place

It was spring. The celebration of the feast of Passover coincided with the celebration of Unleavened Bread. The first feast commemorated Israel's redemption from slavery in Egypt, and most specifically how that final, fateful plague led Pharaoh to drive the people of Israel out of his land. That plague was the death of the firstborn, from which the Israelites were protected by the blood of the lamb. In the centuries thereafter, Passover was observed through a meal, recalling the meal of lamb on which each Israelite household feasted that one decisive night in Egypt.[2]

The second feast—the feast of Unleavened Bread—spans a week. Leaven is to be removed from homes in preparation for the feast and the people abstain from eating leaven for the duration. The preparation for this feast overlaps with Passover and then extends beyond the specific day of Passover. The unleavened bread, of course, recalls what the Israelites prepared and packed for their hasty flight from Egypt. As Luke the Evangelist phrases things, it sounds like these two feasts are the same, whereas they are in fact distinct but coincident, while also resonating with each other in what they commemorate.[3]

---

[2] The actual meal is known as the *Seder*, but I will continue to call it the "Passover meal" to keep the connection to the event of the exodus as clear and vivid as possible for us.

[3] Fred B. Craddock, "Luke," in *The HarperCollins Bible Commentary*, ed. James L. Mays (San Francisco: HarperSanFrancisco, 2000), 952; *The Ignatius Catholic Study Bible: The New Testament* (San Francisco: Ignatius, 2010), 148.

This festal setting draws Israel back to that great event when God freed his people from slavery and sent them out into the desert on their journey to the fullness of freedom. The ancient Israelites were saved from death and brought into new life. They were protected by the blood of the lamb. But on the occasion of this Passover, Luke tells us that the "chief priests and the scribes" are out for blood, seeking to put Jesus to death (22:2).

And so it is during the feast when Israel remembers God's deliverance from death by the blood of the lamb that the religious leaders seek to bring death upon this man, Jesus. In the passage that follows, bread and wine are spoken of, but no lamb. Where is the lamb? Or more to the point, *who* is the lamb?

The twelve apostles are the witnesses who see and hear, feel and taste the answer to that question.

The Offering of Jesus

The narrative of the Last Supper is relatively brief, but the meaning is inexhaustible. Jesus begins by identifying this meal as Passover and ties it to his suffering that will soon begin. That suffering is itself tied back to what we hear at the beginning of the episode—that the chief priests and scribes are seeking his death. Jesus is fully aware of what is taking place around him and because of him. It is this meal, then, that he has longed to share with his apostles and which, as he tells them, he will not eat again until "it is fulfilled in the kingdom of God" (22:16). What this fulfillment means is not entirely clear, but it is worth noting that on the other side of the resurrection, Jesus breaks bread with the two disciples who were bound for Emmaus in a way that clearly connects to what took place at this Last Supper (see Luke 24:30-32). Seen from that perspective, the fulfillment in the kingdom of God begins with the resurrection.[4]

Before Jesus takes the bread, Luke tells us that he takes the chalice. In fact, Luke will speak twice of Jesus taking and offering the chalice (22:17, 20). The Passover meal includes four cups of wine, each with

---

[4] Raymond E. Brown, *An Introduction to the New Testament* (New York: Doubleday, 1997), 256.

its own prayer. The chalice that precedes the meal here in Luke's narrative is either the first or second cup: the first cup is used to sanctify the feast while the second follows the singing of Psalm 114, which recounts the Lord's wonders at the exodus. Indeed, each of the four cups stands for one of the four promises the Lord makes to his people in Exodus:

- "I will free you from the labors of the Egyptians" (6:6a).
- "[I will] deliver you from your bondage" (6:6b).
- "I will redeem you with an outstretched arm" (6:6c).
- "I will take you to be My people, and I will be your God" (6:7a).[5]

The third cup, then, recalls the promise of redemption. This is the cup that immediately follows the meal, which is what Jesus offers with the words: "This cup which is poured out for you is the new covenant in my blood" (Luke 22:20). This new covenant brings redemption, and Jesus' blood is how redemption is won. His is the blood that saves, now and for all time. Those who receive the gift of his blood are delivered not from slavery in Egypt but from sin, redeemed now to inherit eternal life with God.

Preceding the giving of this chalice by which Jesus offers his own blood for the redemption of those who share in it, Jesus takes bread, gives thanks, breaks it, and gives it to his apostles. This fourfold action of taking, blessing, breaking, and giving was already anticipated at the feeding of the five thousand. Unlike that earlier feeding, however, Jesus now identifies this offering with himself in a definitive way: "This is my body which is given for you" (Luke 22:19b). As with the bread of life discourse in John 6, his body is what is given as food, so that those who eat of it may have eternal life. This is the true manna, the true bread come down from heaven. This offering is the center and meaning of everything. When he says, "Do this in memory of me" (22:19b), this now is the event that completes and fulfills what began in the exodus, when God pledged to the people that, for them, he would be liberator, deliverer, redeemer, and their God. As the Israelites were to remember the exodus through the perpetual observance of the Passover feast

---

[5] These lines from Exodus all come from the JPS translation.

(see Deut 16:3), so now all are to live in the memory of Jesus' one sacrifice, who offers himself as the true lamb.[6]

Eternity in Light of Yesterday

What the apostles both witnessed and received at the Last Supper was more than they could fully grasp. Jesus celebrated the Passover with them. Everything he did was according to the form of the Passover meal. When he took and offered the cups, these offerings had meaning according to the event of the exodus in ages past and according to the Jewish traditions of remembering that event as a perpetual institution. Likewise, when he offered the unleavened bread and placed the central focus on the food that he was now giving, there was already a meaning for his apostles according to the memory of the paschal lamb and the unleavened bread of the exodus. And yet, though Jesus observed the Passover feast along with the feast of Unleavened Bread, he was not only observing what a faithful Jew would observe. Rather, in the midst of this observance, he was bringing everything to its fulfillment, as he offered himself—body and blood, soul and divinity—as God's definitive act of redemption for the life of the world.

To "know" what the gift of his body as this bread would mean, the apostles would have to witness and endure his death, and then receive him again as risen from the dead. To "know" the meaning of his blood, they would bear witness to that blood being shed for love of them. Realizing and being grateful for the gift given to them at the Last Supper was not only a matter of having to wait for the subsequent events to take place so they could "get it"; what the apostles needed—and would always need—was to learn how to encounter that bread and wine given to them as the real and eternal presence of the one who loved them to the end. And what those apostles received, they were then commissioned to hand on to others: this one gift of the body and blood of the true lamb, the bread of life, the blood of salvation.

When Jesus gave thanks with the bread he had taken (22:19), his thanks were offered to his Father in heaven. The "giving thanks" that we read in that verse is a translation of the Greek verb *eucharisteō*.[7]

---

[6] Brown, *Introduction to the New Testament*, 256; cf. *Ignatius Catholic Study Bible*, 148–49; and Craddock, "Luke," 952.
[7] *Ignatius Catholic Study Bible*, 149.

The sacrament of the Eucharist takes its name from the thanks that Jesus gave to his Father. To celebrate that sacrament "in memory of" Jesus means entering into the thanks he himself offered to his Father. For what is the Son thankful to the Father? It is more than the apostles or any of us can comprehend. And yet, by giving us his body and his blood, the Son draws us into his thanks to the Father, so his gratitude may become our own.

Guiding Your Child to Engage "Jesus Instituting the Eucharist"

Overview

A Look from Above
In the three episodes from the gospels so far, we have seen Jesus multiplying the bread (and fish) to feed people, turning water into wine for people to drink, and teaching the people that his flesh is true bread and his blood true drink. Now that we come to the Last Supper, all that Jesus has done and said comes to fulfillment. This is where he first gives his body and blood under the appearance of bread and wine. We will see the gift of Jesus' body and blood partly by remembering the Passover (chapter 3).

A Closer Look
Jesus' words and actions at the Last Supper are at the center of every eucharistic liturgy. Here we will listen to those words and see those actions as the fulfillment of the Passover—now from sin to grace, from death to life. Jesus himself is the lamb of God, the bread of life, the one whose blood saves his beloved from death.

1st Movement—Welcoming the Word of God

1. Opening Prayer

2. Quick Review

    Remembering the Passover (Exod 12:1-20) is important for this session. Continue to use your child's drawings for these reviews, if possible. The three key points to be sure to review here are the following:

    - During the Passover, the blood of the lamb protected the Israelites from death.
    - The main meal at the Passover was that same lamb.
    - The unleavened bread that the Israelites prepared fed them for their journey out of slavery and into freedom with God.

Jesus Institutes the Eucharist at the Last Supper   107

You may also quickly review the previous three sessions from the gospels, which all culminate in what Jesus says and does at the Last Supper.

- Jesus fed five thousand people with bread that he took, blessed, broke, and gave.
- Jesus gave drink to the people at Cana with the water he turned into wine.
- Jesus taught the people that he is the bread of life—the true manna—and that his body and blood give eternal life.

2nd *Movement—Engaging the Word of God*

1. Reading

   Luke 22:1-2, 14-20. Read the passage through slowly, out loud.

2. Questions about the Reading

   After you finish reading the passage once, ask the following questions and talk together about each part of this event:

   - Question: When Jesus gathers his disciples for this meal, what holiday are they celebrating?
     - Read 22:1-2 again.
     - Answer: Passover. (Technically, there are two feasts, with the second being the feast of Unleavened Bread, but identifying Passover is the most important.)
     - Follow up: What do you remember about Passover? (This gives a chance for yet another review of the Old Testament episode.)
   - Question: What do people eat at Passover? (May not need to ask if mentioned above.)
     - Answer: Lamb is the main meal. Also, unleavened bread.
   - Question: Let's pay attention to the bread here. What does Jesus do with the bread?
     - Read 22:19 again.

- Answer: He takes it, blesses it (gives thanks), breaks it, and gives it to his apostles saying that *this* bread is his body "given for you."
- Follow up: Do you remember where else Jesus took, blessed, broke, and gave bread to people? (Answer: The feeding of the five thousand.)
- Follow up: What is different here from the feeding of the five thousand? (Answer: Now he says that this bread is his body.)
- Follow up: Since this is a Passover meal, what do you remember about the bread at the Passover? (It was unleavened and it was food for the journey. If Jesus is this bread, then he himself is food for his disciples' journey to heaven.)

- Question: Jesus also does something with the cup of wine, the chalice. What does he do?
  - Read 22:20 again.
  - Answer: He says that this wine is his blood, and it is poured out for his disciples as the new covenant.
  - Follow up: What do you remember about the blood of the lamb from the Passover? (God made the blood protect the Israelites from death.)
  - Teach: Jesus' blood is like that lamb's blood, except Jesus' blood does not just save from slavery and death but brings his disciples into the life of God. That's what the "new covenant" means. It is eternal life with God.

- Question: The Last Supper is a Passover meal and Jesus gives his body with the bread and his blood with the wine, but isn't the main meal at the Passover the lamb? Do we hear anything about a lamb at this meal?
  - Feel free to read the whole passage again, and have your child listen closely.
  - Answer: There is no mention of the lamb.
  - Teach: There is no lamb mentioned because *Jesus is the lamb of God.*

3. Points to Emphasize

   These are some main points to emphasize in summary, at the end:

   - Jesus told the people they had to eat his body and drink his blood to have life with God, but he didn't tell them how. At the Last Supper, he showed his apostles how to eat his body and drink his blood: by the bread and wine of the Eucharist.
   - At the Last Supper, Jesus shows himself as the true bread. He is like the Passover bread, but more. He is like the manna, but more. He is like the bread that fed the five thousand, but more. All those things point to the true bread: Jesus.
   - At the Last Supper, Jesus gives his blood so his disciples may have life with God. His blood is like the blood of the lamb at Passover, but more. He is the true lamb of God.
   - At every Eucharist, we receive what the apostles received at the Last Supper: the body and blood of Jesus.

3rd Movement—Reflecting on the Word of God

1. Activity

   Draw the scene.

2. Discussion

   Ask your child to tell you about the drawing.

3. Closing Prayer

chapter eleven

Jesus Redeems the Two Bound for Emmaus

(Luke 24:13-37)

The two travelers on their way to Emmaus were sad—very sad. They not only looked sad (Luke 24:17) but also confessed that they were without hope. In fact, their hope was in the past tense: "we *had hoped* that he was the one to redeem Israel" (24:21).[1] Whatever hope they had was now firmly behind them as they walked away from Jerusalem, away from the place where Jesus had been killed, away from the good things they had expected.

It is not like one thing or another didn't work out for them. *Everything* had gone wrong. They had placed all their hopes on this man Jesus, with some kind of expectation of what he would do for them and for all of Israel, and now it seemed like all those hopes had come to nothing. That man was dead. Their expectations were unmet. They were returning to their own village with nothing to show for any of it, covered in sadness.

I have known people from time to time who have resembled these two travelers—and to be honest, maybe I have resembled them at times, too. Nothing turned out as I planned. The world is suddenly very different than I thought it would be. God does not seem to be who I

---

[1] Italics added. All biblical quotations in this chapter come from the RSV translation, unless otherwise noted.

thought God was. The meaning for my life is uncertain. I'm heading back to where I started, having gained nothing and lost everything.

This is the condition of the travelers when Jesus comes to them, though of course they do not recognize him. "Their eyes were kept from recognizing him" (24:16). He is not hiding from them—he is there in plain sight, right next to them, talking with them—but there is something about the condition of their eyes that prevents them from seeing and knowing him. What follows is about their transformation as they change from not knowing him to knowing him. This transformation is not something that just happens to them out of nowhere; rather, the transformation is a matter of what Jesus does to them and for them. Jesus turns their sadness into joy.

The Actions of Jesus

The two travelers set the terms for the first part of the journey. They have chosen the destination and they do most of the talking. Jesus is the one who comes to them, asks a question (twice), and listens to them. At the beginning, the travelers seem more active, whereas Jesus is more passive. He is following their lead.

Who is leading changes abruptly as soon as the travelers stop speaking. It may even be that Jesus puts an end to their talking when he calls them "foolish" (24:25). From that point forward, Jesus is the one directing the action, and his actions are decisive, even transformational for the two travelers.

The first action is indeed to silence these two chatty wanderers so that, instead of babbling on about what they do not understand, they might *listen*. Any understanding they come to will follow not from more talking, but first from hearing well. In order to hear, their talking must cease. Jesus is the one who silences them.

The second action is to correct them in their understanding of power. They had thought that "the Christ"—God's anointed one—would be the one who was mightier than all, who beat back those with power by the exercise of even more power. If, for example, Israel was under the control of the Roman Empire, then they expected God's anointed one to be a leader who would defeat the Romans and drive them out. The Messiah they expected would be a more powerful version of all the other rulers they had known, from the Roman Emperor to their corrupt religious authorities.[2] Instead, Jesus begins schooling them with his rhetorical question: "Was it not necessary that the Christ should suffer these things and enter into his glory?" (24:26). They had imagined a god who was a more powerful version of all the power figures they knew—one who happened to be on their side—rather than recognizing the God of Israel as the one who is willing to suffer with and for his people out of love. The glory of God and of his Christ is in humility.[3]

The third action is to renew and rebuild their understanding of Scripture. Their errant expectations—which had also blinded them to Jesus' presence—were based on misinterpreting the Scriptures. We could perhaps understand this if we think about going to the Bible to find what we already wanted to find, as opposed to going to the Bible to discover God for who God is. In the first instance, you already have criteria for what is acceptable and what is not—as if "God has to be this way" or "this is what is fair and just" or "the world is obviously about this and not that." In the second instance, you are willing to examine and reconsider even what you assumed might be true and certain based on who God shows himself to be and how God acts in history. If, for example, you begin by assuming that God must just be a stronger version of every other kind of ruler you have encountered, then you will very likely find what you want to find to support the idea you already had. What Jesus does for them is begin again from the beginning: "beginning with Moses and all the prophets, he interpreted to them in all the scriptures the things concerning himself" (24:27). Knowing the Christ for who he is requires learning from Scripture—in fact, it requires opening yourself to all of Scripture.

Fourth and finally, Jesus feeds them and thus enkindles within the zeal of a new mission. This last action completes and builds on the

---

[2] A litany of these power brokers is provided earlier in Luke's gospel, specifically in 3:1-2. For a marvelous reflection on this passage of Luke's gospel in relation to the overturning of power that is taking place in the coming of Christ, see Alfred Delp, *Advent of the Heart: Seasonal Sermons and Prison Writings, 1941–1944* (San Francisco: Ignatius, 2006), 128–30.

[3] This reversal of power is at the heart of St. Paul's memorable lines in 1 Cor 1:24-25, where Christ is named as the power and wisdom of God, but not according to how the world measures either power or wisdom.

other three. Once again, the Lord feeds his people. This last action invites us to grow in our understanding, appreciation, and gratitude for who the Lord is and what the Lord does for us.

The Meal Under Their Roof

"When [Jesus] was at table with them, he took the bread . . ." (24:30). Even in an incredible narrative like this one, it is easy to get lulled into complacency, thinking to yourself "I know what is going on here." It seems natural—almost expected—for Jesus to be "at table" and for him to do something with the bread. But perhaps we have not marveled long enough at this fact: the table at which Jesus was sitting was not his table, nor was the bread his bread. In fact, the house in which he now dwells is not his house. The table at which Jesus sits is the table of those two travelers, the bread is their bread, and Jesus is in *their* house because they invited him in. "He appeared to be going further, but they constrained him, saying, 'Stay with us, for it is toward evening and the day is now far spent.' So he went in to stay with them" (24:28-29).

Jesus does not force his way in; he responds to their invitation. They bring him in, they set the table, they provide the bread. What Jesus does for them he does in response to their hospitality. He takes their bread "and blessed and broke it, and gave it to them" (24:30). He gives them back what they gave to him, but what they receive back is not unchanged; indeed, it is *substantially* changed. By his gift of bread they recognize *him*: "he was made known to them in the breaking of the bread" (24:35).

It is worth thinking back over the entire narrative to try to grasp what happens in this exchange of bread. What did these two travelers give to Jesus, from beginning to end? They gave him their many words, their confusion, their hopelessness, their aimlessness. After he taught them, they then gave him their hospitality, welcoming him into their home, under their roof. Jesus accepts it all: the good, the bad, the uncertain, the generous. He takes all they give and gives them back all he has, all he is. He gives them himself.

There are four actions of Jesus in this narrative as a whole, after he draws near to walk with them: he silences them, he corrects them, he opens the Scriptures to them, and he feeds them with the bread of his hands. Within that fourth and final action, however, there is that familiar fourfold action from the Last Supper: he takes, blesses, breaks, and gives. What Jesus does at their table is what he did at the table in the upper room, where he offered his body and blood to his apostles in the Passover meal. This offering is the continuation of that previous offering—it is all one offering: the offering of his body and his blood, his sacrifice, the love of God poured out for the life of the world.

Seeing the whole narrative of this journey to Emmaus again, perhaps we can notice another pattern being established. Prior to arriving at the travelers' home, Jesus proclaims his identity and mission to them by schooling them in his suffering and opening the Scriptures to them. Then, upon arriving at their home where he comes to take hold of the bread on their table, Jesus blesses, breaks, and gives to them the food that changes them. First, then, there is the proclamation from Scripture, then there is the feeding from the table. These are the two liturgies of the Mass: the Liturgy of the Word (the reading of Scripture) and the Liturgy of the Eucharist. Jesus was not following the Mass; the Mass follows what Jesus does with and for his disciples, with and for the Church. This also shows us what is required of those who seek Jesus in the Eucharist: we ought to bring everything to him, we ought to open ourselves to the word of God in Scripture, and we ought to each invite him to come "under my roof."

Renewed from this entire encounter—the encounter with Jesus in word and sacrament: in Scripture and in the breaking of the bread—the disciples' "hearts burn within" them and they arise immediately with zeal in a new mission. They go back to where they had just come from—Jerusalem—to bring good news to the others. They are filled with the mission of the Gospel. In other words, "Go forth, the Mass is ended." "Go and announce the Gospel of the Lord."

Like Weary Prophets

When Jesus came upon those weary and hopeless travelers, they were not unlike that exhausted and exasperated prophet Elijah, who fled to the desert and prayed that the Lord might take his life. While he was in that desperate state, the angel of the Lord came to the prophet to rouse him, strengthen him with food, and refresh him with drink. Twice the angel did this. By the power of what he received, Elijah journeyed much further into the wilderness toward Horeb.

After powers of earth and sky passed him by, Elijah encountered the Lord himself in a tiny whispering sound—a sound of total stillness. He knew the Lord in that gentle but sure approach. When Elijah gave all that he had to the Lord, including the account of his own zeal along with his own anxiety and despondency, the Lord gave him a new mission in response. Changed by his encounter with the Lord, Elijah went back to the land he had fled and carried out the Lord's commands, obedient to his every word.

What Elijah encountered in silence on the mountain, the two travelers encountered in person at Emmaus. The silent and sure presence of God was unveiled for them in the glorified flesh and then the sacramental bread of Jesus, the Christ. Receiving him, they received newness of life—they received Joy.

Guiding Your Child to Engage "Jesus at Emmaus"

Overview

A Look from Above
This episode and the following one are both narratives of Jesus' resurrection appearances. The Old Testament connection we will invite here is with the weary prophet Elijah, who was strengthened by the bread of the angel and journeyed far to meet the Lord in silence (chapter 5).

A Closer Look
Like all of the resurrection appearance narratives, the disciples here do not recognize Jesus at first. Only when Jesus teaches them and finally gives himself to them in "the breaking of the bread" do they know and accept Jesus for who he is. This particular narrative also establishes the shape of Mass, moving from the Liturgy of the Word (verses 25-27) to the Liturgy of the Eucharist (verses 28-31), even unto the dismissal filled with the mission of the Lord (verses 32-35). As for the condition of the disciples, their movement from deep sadness to splendid joy is reminiscent of the prophet Elijah in 1 Kings 19.

1st Movement—Welcoming the Word of God

1. Opening Prayer

2. Quick Review

    Recall what immediately preceded this session in our journey, which is the Last Supper (Luke 22:1-2, 14-20). Some keys points include the following:

    - The Last Supper is a Passover meal and Jesus is the lamb of God.

    - Jesus offers his body to the disciples in the bread.

    - Jesus offers his blood to the disciples through the wine. His blood is what gives everyone life with God, just like the paschal lamb's blood saved the Israelites from death.

Additionally, it is helpful to recall the narrative of the prophet Elijah in 1 Kings 19, using your child's drawing if possible. These three key points are important:

- Elijah began without hope—very sad and tired.
- An angel came to Elijah to give him bread and water, which strengthened Elijah.
- Elijah met God in the silence on Mount Horeb, and God gave Elijah a new mission.

2nd Movement—Engaging the Word of God

1. Reading in Three Parts, with Discussion. (Be sure to note that it is the day of Jesus' resurrection from the dead.)
   - Part 1: The Condition of the Travelers (Luke 24:13-17)
     - Read Luke 24:13-17. Ask: What are these two travelers like when Jesus meets them? Are they happy, sad, or what?
       - Answer: They are sad (see 24:17).
       - Teach: Show your child that they do not recognize Jesus (24:16). Be sure to stress that this is *not* because Jesus is disguised but rather because the disciples were not yet ready to believe in Jesus' resurrection.
     - Show your child why these two travelers are sad by reading Luke 24:18-24.
       - Teach: See how the travelers believed Jesus was a prophet like other prophets, but that is all (24:19-20).
       - Teach: See how they *had hoped* in him, but do not hope anymore because he has been killed (24:20-21).
       - Teach: See how they have heard that Jesus' body is not in the tomb where they laid him, and yet they do not know what this means, so they are confused in addition to being sad (24:22-24).
   - Part 2: What Jesus Does (Luke 24:25-30)
     - Ask your child to pay attention to what Jesus does after he listens to these two travelers as you read Luke 24:25-30.

- Let your child tell you what he or she heard about what Jesus does.
- Teach: Help your child see that Jesus teaches these disciples the Scriptures (the Bible). He is teaching them the Old Testament. This is just like what we have been doing. It is important to know the Old Testament so we can really know Jesus (24:25-27).
- Teach: Make sure your child recognizes the fourfold action of Jesus with the bread: "he *took* the bread and *blessed* and *broke* it, and *gave* it to them" (24:30). This is exactly what he did at the Last Supper (and also in the feeding of the five thousand).
- Teach: The two main things Jesus does are teach the disciples the Scriptures and feed them the bread he has taken, blessed, broken, and given.

- Part 3: The Renewal of Mission (Luke 24:31-35)
  - Ask your child to pay attention to what happens to these two disciples after Jesus gives them the bread as you read Luke 24:31-35.
    - Let your child tell you what he or she noticed.
    - Teach: First, when they received the bread from Jesus they immediately recognized him. This shows us that we meet Jesus in the Eucharist (24:31, 35).
    - Teach: Second, they now find great joy in the Scriptures once they recognize Jesus: "our hearts burn within us" (24:32). Jesus shows us the good news of God's love in the Bible.
    - Teach: Third, they have a new mission to tell the good news of Jesus, and they run to do it (24:33-35).

2. Points to Emphasize

   Looking back at this entire narrative, it would be helpful to summarize some key points together:

   - Just like the prophet Elijah, the two travelers that Jesus meets are sad, without hope, and confused.

- After Jesus listens to them, he then teaches them the Scriptures and feeds them with the bread that he has taken, blessed, broken, and given.
- The bread that Jesus gives them is the Eucharist: this is how they know him.
- Just like the prophet Elijah, after these disciples meet Jesus and receive him in the Eucharist they rush out with a new mission. Jesus has turned their sorrow to joy.
- What happened to these two disciples is what Jesus wants to happen to us at every Mass.

3rd Movement—Reflecting on the Word of God

1. Activity

   Draw the scene.

2. Discussion

   Ask your child to tell you about the drawing.

3. Closing Prayer

chapter twelve

Jesus Renews His Disciples on the Seashore

(John 21:1-14)

In the 1991 film *Hook* starring Robin Williams, Peter Pan returns to the Lost Boys in Neverland after a long absence. The boy who never grows up has, by this point, actually grown up. The youthful and mischievous Peter Pan has become the hyper-rational and cautious Peter Banning, a corporate lawyer. The Lost Boys do not recognize this dull man as their long-lost leader. But then something changes. While they are sitting together at an empty table "eating" food that isn't really there, Peter suddenly does what he used to do: he makes it all real. By his act of imagination and the force of his rediscovered charisma, a sumptuous feast appears before them. Only then do the Lost Boys recognize Peter for who he is.

Jesus Christ is not Peter Pan. Though he was separated from his disciples for three days, Jesus did not go away to get dull and lose who he really was. He is not a conjurer of the imagination who turns make-believe into reality. His power is not merely the power of imagination and charisma. In one important respect, though, what happens with Jesus Christ is mirrored in the revelation of Peter Pan in *Hook*: his followers recognize him for who he is because they witness what he does. Jesus' identity is made evident through his actions.

Who do the disciples eventually recognize on the seashore? They recognize the Lord. The one who called and fed them before, calls and feeds them now. That's just who he is.

Back to the Ordinary, and Back Again

"I am going fishing" (John 21:3).[1] Simon Peter was a fisherman before the Lord called him. Now that the Lord is seemingly no longer with his disciples, Simon Peter goes back to what he did before. The others go with him. And just like it was on the night before Jesus called them as disciples, these fishermen catch nothing. Their labors are fruitless.[2]

Then dawn breaks. That is the moment when Jesus appeared on the shore and called to them, though they did not recognize him. Right from the start, he is presented as the one who dispels the darkness (see John 1:4-5), like the sun itself which rises swiftly in the East. "Cast the net on the right side of the boat, and you will find some [fish]" (John 21:6; cf. Luke 3:4), this unrecognizable stranger tells them. They do what he says, and no sooner do they heed his command—as senseless as it seemed—than their nets are so overstuffed that they cannot haul them in.

At that moment, at the break of dawn, with the nets filled to the point of bursting, the first flash of recognition strikes the Beloved Disciple, John: "It is the Lord!" (21:7). The man on the seashore was not previously invisible—they all saw him just as they all heard him. And yet laying eyes on him was not the same as *seeing* him for who he truly is. Once he acts toward them in the way they had known him to act before, they start to recognize him. It is not at all by accident that the first one to *see* is the one who is known as the "beloved." Love sees further.

Simon Peter, whose plan it was to go fishing in the first place, is the first to abandon those plans the moment he hears that it is indeed the Lord who stands on the seashore. He jumps in the water and swims to shore, while the others come in by boat. Before he met the Lord, Simon Peter was a fisherman. When he thought the Lord absent, he went back to fishing. Now that he hears the Lord is alive and calling to him again, he makes haste to return to the Lord.

The Lord called Simon Peter and the others in just the way in which they would recognize him. He appealed to their memories of their first

---

[1] All biblical quotations in this chapter come from the RSV translation, unless otherwise noted.

[2] For the original call narrative, see Luke 5:3-7.

calling, so that he could fulfill now what he began in them from the start. He is drawing them to himself.

The Substance of Things Hoped For

When the disciples arrived at shore, food was already prepared for them. Jesus himself had prepared the fish and provided bread. Where did this fish and bread come from? They are not told, nor are we. It is just provided; Jesus is the one who provides it. And yet, he also invites or commands them to bring what they have caught and add it to what he provides. Even what they themselves can now add to this meal is what Jesus himself made possible for them to catch. Whether in terms of the food that was waiting for them or the fish that they add to the meal, Jesus' offering comes first. What they offer depends on what he offers, and yet he lets them share in his offering by offering what they have. All of it will be given back to them for their benefit.

"Come and have breakfast" (21:12). This meal of fish and bread by the seashore is reminiscent of the feeding of the five thousand. These disciples saw him feed others with abundance out of scarcity then, and now they see him feeding them with abundance following their fruitless nighttime labors out at sea. None of them ask him who he is, for they have no need to ask: "They knew it was the Lord" (21:12). They do not just see the food; they see him who feeds them. They know themselves as the ones whom he feeds, and they know him as the one who always feeds them. This is who he is: their shepherd. You cannot recognize that without gratitude, without love.

Jesus' final action in this part of the episode is stated in specific detail: "Jesus came and took the bread and gave it to them, and so with the fish" (21:13). Though the fish seemed like the main meal and that to which the disciples added their own, the bread is mentioned by name here as that which he *took and gave to them*. In the Last Supper narratives—which John's gospel lacks, at least in terms of the consecration of the bread and wine—the fourfold action of Jesus is to take, bless, break, and give the bread (Luke 22:19; Matt 26:26; Mark 14:22). That fourfold action is repeated in Emmaus (Luke 24:30). Here on the seashore, Jesus does not just invite them to come eat what they want; instead, he himself takes the bread and gives it to them. The bread they receive is not just bread, but bread given. It is the bread that he gives. This is all about the question of who feeds. Jesus is the Lord, the one who feeds.

Out of the Garden, and Back Again

The world as God created it is a place full of what would nourish and delight us, God's creatures. We are not placed in a world that lacks what we need, that is marked by scarcity, or that is hostile to us. We are not created to languish but to live. God creates us and God creates the conditions for us to live abundantly.

This is the image that is presented in the Garden of Eden, in which the "Lord God caused to grow every tree that was pleasing to the sight and good for food" (Gen 2:9, JPS). Our fallen world—the world marred by sin, selfishness, and our lack of care for one another—is often a harsh world, an empty world, a fruitless world. Like the disciples alone at night on the seashore, our labors in such a world often come to naught. But that is not the world as God created it. His world is a world of abundant life.

What happens on the seashore is a return to God's world, through Jesus Christ, risen from the dead. The life that he opens to his disciples is God's own life, where food emerges from lack, fullness from scarcity, generosity from fear. Jesus *gives* the bread and the disciples *receive* what he gives; they do not take. From the start, sin was a failure to receive what the Lord gives, choosing to take what (you think) you want instead. But on the other side of the resurrection, the Lord calls his disciples to himself and forms them to receive anew. He gives himself to them freely; they receive him freely. They do not doubt but know that he is who he has shown himself to be. He is the Tree of Life.

Guiding Your Child to Engage "Jesus on the Seashore"

Overview

A Look from Above

This final episode of our journey is also a resurrection appearance narrative. Jesus has appeared to his disciples several times, and yet here they do not recognize him again. There is always a change that must take place in the disciples to see and know Jesus as he is in glory. The Old Testament connection we will keep in view is with the goodness of the Garden of Eden in Genesis 2 (chapter 1).

A Closer Look

Even though they have met the Lord previously in his resurrection, several of the apostles return to what they were doing before Jesus called them in the first place: fishing. Just like then, they are totally unsuccessful in fishing now . . . until Jesus comes to them. It will be helpful (as noted below) to talk with your child about the calling of Peter in Luke 5:1-11, since this narrative evokes it.

1ˢᵗ Movement—Welcoming the Word of God

1. Opening Prayer

2. Quick Review

   It is helpful to remember Genesis 2, where the man the Lord God creates is placed in an abundant garden (chapter 1). The key points are these:

   - The garden shows us the world God creates for human beings: it is filled with gifts and is a place for us to live with him.

   - To receive gifts, we open our hands (remember the posture, like that for receiving the Eucharist).

   - In the middle of the garden were two trees: the tree of knowledge of good and bad, and the tree of life. Adam and Eve pay attention to the tree of knowledge of good and bad, which they were told not to do. The tree of life, however, was overlooked.

   If necessary, recall the Last Supper narrative (Luke 22:1-2, 14-20).

2nd *Movement—Engaging the Word of God*

1. Reading in Three Parts, with Discussion. (Be sure to note that this is another story about Jesus meeting his disciples after the resurrection.)
   - Part 1: What the Disciples are Doing (John 21:1-3)
     - Read John 21:1-3. Ask: What are the disciples doing?
       - Answer: They are fishing.
       - Ask: Are they catching any fish?
       - Answer: No.
       - Teach: This is just like what Peter and some of the other disciples were doing right before Jesus called them to follow him (see Luke 5:1-11).
   - Part 2: How Jesus Changes Things (John 21:4-8)
     - Read John 21:4-6. Ask: What does Jesus tell them and what happens when they do what he tells them?
       - Answer: Jesus tells them to put their nets on the other side of the boat. When they do what Jesus tells them, their nets fill with fish.
       - Teach: Again, this is what happened when Jesus called Peter.
       - Teach: John (the Beloved Disciple) and then Peter recognize Jesus once they see him do what he did before (24:7).
   - Part 3: How Jesus Fed Them (John 21:9-14)
     - Ask your child to pay attention to what happens when the disciples meet Jesus on the shore as you read John 21:9-14.
       - Let your child tell you what he or she noticed.
       - Teach: Notice that Jesus has food for them when they arrive. He has fish and bread (21:9). That is the same food as the feeding of the five thousand.
       - Teach: Help your child to see that even though Jesus has food for them, he invites them to add the fish they caught to the meal (21:10-11).

- Teach: See that the disciples *know* Jesus when he feeds them (21:12). In fact, Jesus "took the bread and gave it to them" (21:13) which is like the Last Supper.
- Teach: Without Jesus the disciples had nothing (no fish), but when they listen to Jesus and join him, he fills them with all good things.

2. Points to Emphasize

   Looking back at this entire narrative, it would be helpful to summarize some key points together:

   - In the beginning, God placed human beings in a garden where they would receive all they needed. From Jesus, the disciples receive all they need. He feeds them.
   - The disciples first recognize Jesus because they know what he did in the past and they see him doing it again now (filling their nets, feeding them).
   - Without Jesus there is no life. With Jesus, there is everlasting life.

3rd Movement—Reflecting on the Word of God

1. Activity

   Draw the scene.

2. Discussion

   Ask your child to tell you about the drawing.

3. Closing Prayer

Epilogue

This journey through Scripture with the Lord who feeds us began, for me, with my son Josiah as he was preparing to receive his First Communion. By the time you read this, Josiah's younger brother, Isaac, will have received his First Communion, after we shared time together praying with, talking about, and drawing these same twelve episodes. Shortly thereafter, Gianna and then Siena, the youngest of our six kids, will do the same. My hope for each of them is that they will never forget—even when other things in their life might make believing difficult—that every time they approach the altar, the Lord gives himself to them as their food and their drink, so that they may have life.

At the end of your journey alongside your child, I hope that both of you have found a deeper wonder and gratitude for the Lord who feeds us. If you have been creating the drawings of the twelve episodes as you go along, I recommend bringing them together into a book or framing them together like a poster. Those drawings and the scriptural memories they represent are windows into the love of God.

The love of God does not stay far away; he draws near. Near enough for us to touch, near enough for us to taste. There is no greater gift we can give our children than the means to place all their trust in the Lord. The Lord will reward that trust again and again by feeding our children, just as he nourishes us with the gift of his body and his blood.

Printed in April 2023
by Rotomail Italia S.p.A., Vignate (MI) - Italy